positioned for
MIRACLES

Making your life an amazing story

ENDORSEMENTS

"Jerry and Julie are people who walk in the Spirit and are great at being led by the Spirit as they minister daily. I have heard of great revivals they have been part of in Indonesia and the Pacific Islands in the recent past. My heart is in full expectation to both witness and partner with them in their great ministry followed with signs, great wonders and awesome miracles.

"Jerry writes this book not out of borrowed ideas and information. He rather talks heart to heart about what he is personally experiencing daily. His intention for writing is very clear. It's not to 'show off' but to rejoice with us and to teach and motivate us to move in the same unction and anointing. I am greatly blessed by this writing. You will find it difficult to put this book down once you start reading it. I advise you to do it in one sitting. I recommend this book for edification, motivation and Holy Ghost inspiration."

Dr. Leslie Keegel
Foursquare National Leader, Sri Lanka
Co-chair, Foursquare Global Council

Endorsements

"I'm so grateful for my decades-long friendship with Jerry and Julie Stott and I have long-awaited this book. As Jerry ministered as a pastor and now as a missionary, God worked and continues to work in supernatural ways resulting in healings, deliverance, signs, and wonders. I am personally aware of some of what you will read from Jerry's pastoral ministry. I have been with some of those in other nations whose stories you will read and I have met with leaders and some converts of the miracle conversion of the John Frum Cargo Cult. I'm convinced that Jerry has much to teach us as he shares the glorious, the confusing, the frustrating, and the embarrassing in his pursuit of God's miracle-working power—yet you will find that he does so with vulnerability and wonder. My prayer is simple: May this book encourage each one of us to pursue a deeper personal relationship with God; may each of us have greater faith for miracles of healing, repentance, and deliverance; and may we make room and give opportunity for God to supernaturally work among the people we serve, whenever and however we gather."

Dr. James C. Scott Jr.
Director, Foursquare Missions International
Vice President, Foursquare Global Church Operations

Endorsements

"Do we live in days of the miraculous? Yes! We most certainly do and Dr. Jerry Stott has much to share with us. God has called Jerry to experience and minister His miraculous touch to thousands in many nations. Jerry is a trusted and personal friend and I'm so glad that he is sharing with us not only inspiring and encouraging stories, but also practical advice on how each of us might position ourselves so that God, the miracle worker, may supernaturally transform others through us. Please receive my friend, Dr. Jerry, as a friend, teacher, and prompter as he walks with you in this important book."

Dr. Ted Vail
Associate Director of Foursquare Missions International

"It's been said, 'Show me your friends and I'll show you your past, present and your future.' I've known Jerry since 2004 when we first were introduced to one another in Canberra, Australia where we both were speaking at a Foursquare conference. Since then, my wife Lisa and I consider Jerry and Julie Stott some of our dearest friends.

"Every time I get around Jerry, he's sharing about an outpouring of the Holy Spirit on hundreds of teenagers in Indonesia, or a miraculous encounter amongst indigenous tribes in a remote village that civilization and time have forgotten, or a dead man being raised to life. The Spirit's miraculous power seems to follow Jerry everywhere he goes and it inspires me to want to contend for nothing less.

"That's why I am so excited about this book—because he is finally putting to paper all that he has seen and done and is sharing this with us. I'm sure this book will be just a "Part 1" because there will be much more to write in the days and years to come, because I believe Jesus is just getting started with Jerry and Julie. I'm so honored to call them friends!"

Rev. Mike Kai
Senior Pastor, Inspire Church Hawaii

"If you want miracles to happen in your life and ministry, *Positioned for Miracles* was written for you! In this magnificently-woven written tapestry of scriptural teaching, effective demonstration, and transparent emotion, Dr. Jerry Stott clearly presents what it takes to live a life of miracles. From the practical to the spiritual, and from the human to the supernatural, this book will both convince you that God wants every believer to receive and minister in power, and teach you how to make the necessary changes to release the power of God. When we first became senior pastors, Jerry Stott was our overseer. The church that he and Julie pastored was known for healings and miracles, so we're not surprised that these signs followed them onto the mission field. But we also want to affirm that Jerry and Julie are people of character. They practice what they preach, serve humbly, and exude God's love for people. We highly recommend *Positioned for Miracles.*"

Rev. Jerry and Kimberly Dirmann
Senior Pastors, The Rock, a multi-site Foursquare church based in Anaheim, California. Kimberly also serves as the Supervisor of the Southwest District of Foursquare Churches

---

"It has been our privilege to work on this project with our good friend Dr. Jerry Stott. Even as active missionaries living in Papua New Guinea, our lives have been impacted and our faith challenged to believe for greater manifestations of the power of God. As we helped edit the original text, the truths presented constantly reinforced our faith and commitment to serve God in the power of the Holy Spirit. Through true stories and biblical examples Dr. Stott has managed to highlight key principles that position us for miracles. It would be hard to read this book without being challenged to a higher level of faith and expectation."

Drs. Steve and Brooke Highlander
Founders of Christianity in the Third Millennium (C3M) Ministries

Endorsements

"I have just finished reading this book and can't wait to read it a second and third time. Because I have known Jerry and Julie as well as their children for over 20 years, I can wholeheartedly tell you that these stories are real and their love for this subject is infectious. I love how the book is filled with scripture, personal stories, teachings and how Jerry's honest thoughts and real personality comes through his writing. Jerry is a passionate and sensitive man that loves Jesus and wants the Church to know Him and ALL the power of the Holy Spirit. Rarely can Jerry speak of these things without tears flowing down his cheeks. Thank you Jerry and Julie for sharing your life, heart and passion with so many. We are honored to serve Jesus with you for such a time as this! Thank you for this book!!"

Rev. Melinda Scott
Assistant to the Director,
Foursquare Missions International

Positioned for Miracles

Copyright 2015, Dr. J. M. Stott all rights reserved

Published by Foursquare Missions Press

Unless otherwise indicated, all Scripture quotations are taken from the New American Standard Bible®, Copyright © 1960, 1962, 1963, 1968, 1971, 1972, 1973, 1975, 1977, 1995 by The Lockman Foundation. Used by permission. (www.Lockman.org)

Scripture quotations marked (NIV) are taken from the Holy Bible, New International Version®, NIV®. Copyright © 1973, 1978, 1984, 2011 by Biblica, Inc.™ Used by permission of Zondervan. All rights reserved worldwide. (www.zondervan.com) The "NIV" and "New International Version" are trademarks registered in the United States Patent and Trademark Office by Biblica, Inc.™

Scripture quotations marked (AMP) are taken from the Amplified Bible, Copyright © 1954, 1958, 1962, 1964, 1965, 1987 by The Lockman Foundation. Used by permission.

Cover Design: Bob Hunt and Wyce Ghiacy

ISBN: 978-0-692-53152-5

Printed in the United States

Foreword by Dr. Glenn Burris Jr.
President of The Foursquare Church

positioned for MIRACLES

Making your life an amazing story
Dr. Jerry Stott

Copyright 2015, Dr. J. M. Stott all rights reserved
Published by Foursquare Missions Press

DEDICATION

Positioned for Miracles is dedicated to my wife, Julie. Her love, patience, and encouragement toward the writing of this book kept me going from start to finish. We've had a lifetime of miracles together! Thank you, Julie, for your inspiration and dedication.

TABLE OF CONTENTS

FOREWORD	**19**
ACKNOWLEDGMENTS	**23**
AN IMPORTANT WORD FROM THE AUTHOR	**27**
INTRODUCTION	**33**

Chapter 1
THE GREATEST MIRACLE — **39**

Chapter 2
THE POSITION OF HUMILITY
Miracle Ingredient 1 of 7: Bring It to Him — **49**

Chapter 3
THE POSITION OF OBEDIENCE
Miracle Ingredient 2 of 7: Do as He Says — **61**

Chapter 4
THE POSITION OF GIVING
Miracle Ingredient 3 of 7: Give Him What You Have — **73**

Chapter 5
THE POSITION OF RECEIVING
Miracle Ingredient 4 of 7: Keep Full of the Word and Spirit — **87**

Chapter 6
THE POSITION OF EXPECTING
Miracle Ingredient 5 of 7: Consider Your Miracle Is On Its Way **101**

Chapter 7
THE POSITION OF BELIEVING
Miracle Ingredient 6 of 7: Add a Measure of Faith **111**

Chapter 8
THE POSITION OF SERVING
Miracle Ingredient 7 of 7: Mix in Some Compassion **127**

Chapter 9
SEVEN KEYS TO GREATER FAITH – PART 1
Where Faith Comes From **137**

Chapter 10
SEVEN KEYS TO GREATER FAITH – PART 2
Things You Can Do to Build Your Faith **153**

Chapter 11
THE POWER OF PRAYING IN THE HOLY SPIRIT **169**

Chapter 12
RECEIVING THE INCREDIBLE GIFT OF TONGUES **189**

ABOUT THE PUBLISHER **205**

FOREWORD

Positioned for Miracles has come to us right on time! In this contemporary age of uncertainty and global unrest, Dr. Jerry Stott profoundly states that, *"God is calling His Church to arise, to awaken from its slumber."*

The need for divine intervention in our nation and world is at a critical level, and we as believers must begin to recognize the vital partnership we have *by God's design* to become His conduits of grace and healing. In this remarkable and insightful book, Dr. Stott gives us both the spiritual principles and the practical steps we all need in order to be *"Positioned for Miracles."*

Drawn from the Gospel of John, Chapter 2, we are given seven principles that enable us to become an empowered people who see the release of God's Spirit at work to transform circumstances and individual lives. Beginning with The Position of *Humility* and moving through each of the other six *miracle ingredients* (as the author calls them), we become immersed in truth and instructed well in these vital principles—*Humility, Obedience, Giving, Receiving, Expecting, Believing* and *Serving.*

The following statement particularly struck me, *"Being 'positioned' for miracles in your life is ultimately about a lifestyle. You can't turn it on and off. You must decide if you want to live a life that sees God do Kingdom of God, in the words of the late John Wimber, 'stuff.' You must desire to walk in faith, live a life pleasing to Him, and be willing to risk, even fail. There is no secret formula."*

I have known Dr. Jerry Stott for a number of years and have always been impacted by his passion and his vision for the lost. In this book, he shares with us many personal accounts that testify of his walk, his struggles, and his victories *because* of God's powerful intervention in his own life and in the life of those he serves. It is his openly transparent communication about his own journey that drew me instantly to identify with him and, thus, to consider my own walk of faith and quest for a Spirit-empowered life.

It is the poignant awareness quickened by the Holy Spirit that draws us ever closer to Christ and His divine call. All miracles – every miraculous intervention – are sovereign acts that bring Heaven to earth; it is God's divine design. AND one of the greatest miracles is that it is HIS purposed plan to bring us into this redemption story—first, to be redeemed, then, to become His agents of miraculous intervention!

This book is about the miraculous intervention of God *and* about our purposed partnership in the grand design of Kingdom transformation on this earth.

In closing, it must not go without mention that Dr. Jerry Stott personifies the qualities and miracle ingredients about which he speaks. Proverbs 4:23 is the scripture verse that comes to mind when I think of his life and testimony and speaks of his integrity: *"Above all else, guard your heart, for everything you do flows from it."* (NIV)

This book is the outcome, and we are richer for it!

                    Glenn C. Burris, Jr.
                    President, The Foursquare Church
                    August 18, 2015

ACKNOWLEDGMENTS

A very special thanks to Drs. Steve and Brooke Highlander. Your tireless encouragement, thoughts, edits, and constant input have made Positioned for Miracles possible. We are grateful beyond measure.

To my dear friend Bob Hunt and the incredible team at Foursquare Missions Press (FMP), a very special thanks. Bob, for your friendship, constant encouragement, suggestions, additions, extraordinary writing and editing skills, that have not only added to the richness of this book but brought it to heights I had never even dreamed of. I want to express my deepest gratitude and immeasurable appreciation for your professionalism and driven passion to bring the Foursquare Gospel to the world. This has truly been an overwhelming blessing to all of us and the millions that have received the Gospel through the tireless efforts of FMP.

To Laurie Gerdes and Wyce Ghiacy, your hard work and love for this project is beyond evident in every page that your time and hands have touched. You are both so appreciated as partners in this project and partners in the ministry to the countless souls that will find a new level of faith and walk with Jesus because of this book.

Working on *Positioned for Miracles* with the FMP Five Star team of professionals has given me a clearer picture of how a dream like this can become a reality. What a joy it has been to work with godly people operating in their gifting and coming together as one with a purpose for the Kingdom. It is just like the Psalm 133 blessing and anointing that comes when we work together in unity "for there the Lord has commanded the blessing." I truly believe the touch of the Holy Spirit was upon us all during this project and it has been absolutely wonderful to have that touch during this first hand experience. No doubt Heaven will have multitudes singing His praise because of the unselfish love you have all given. May the Holy Spirit breathe life on every FMP resource as the gospel finds its way to every village, tribe, language and people group throughout the world.

AN IMPORTANT WORD FROM THE AUTHOR

This book is essentially about moving in the power of the Holy Spirit. I've focused on the passage in John 2 and have extracted seven principles that I truly believe will help the reader walk in that power.

In doing so, I'm very aware that principles, in and of themselves, should never substitute for living in the manifest presence of the Lord. Principles, especially those I've listed in context to the Scripture, only serve as guides—hopefully moving us back to that presence. In the intimacy of marriage I must continually be in the presence of my wife; but there are principles, that if I follow, will lead me to a deeper love.

Adding to that illustration, living in my wife's presence and following biblical principles of marriage will allow me to be increasingly sensitive to her and to her needs. In the presence of the Spirit we too can "see that which the Spirit is saying." But if we disregard various principles of Spirit living, the relationship will suffer and our spiritual clarity will cloud.

When I've seen people healed and had a specific word for them beforehand I was being guided by a Person and was in

His Presence. Yet I also was moving according to biblical truths and principles—the two never contradict.

The challenge writers face, especially in describing things of the Spirit, is that books by their very nature tend toward the cognitive. Life in the Spirit also involves the mind but in perfect harmony with our soul and spirit.

My prayer is that this book will inform and inspire but, most of all, drive you to that deeper place, into a more intimate relationship with Jesus our Lord.

To contact Jerry and to read and see more
of what the Lord is doing around the world go to
www.positionedformiracles.com

positioned for MIRACLES

Making your life an amazing story

INTRODUCTION

I won't deny it was exciting—being driven through the crowded streets of Mindoro, Philippines with huge banners colorfully scraping the skyline proclaiming the crusade.

Bicycles darted between cars, avoiding people spilling from the sidewalks. My head swiveled catching the lights and sights, only being distracted by the men talking rapidly with bullhorns while driving motorbikes. They announced the meeting that would be held that night.

And I was the main attraction.

What a speaker never wants is to be distracted just before he or she goes out on stage. Adrenaline properly mixed with prayer provides powerful focus. Take that away and your emotions can run away on the next bus. In this case, the metaphor was actual—a bus full of children.

One by one, the children, some teenagers, were assisted off the bus. They were led to the front of the stage.

> *B*eing "positioned" for miracles in your life is ultimately about a lifestyle. You can't turn it on and off.

My friend, Pastor Joe Danganan (Founder of PCF churches in the Philippines, USA and Canada), as if on cue, went to the microphone and pronounced in a nearly matter of fact tone, "Pastor Jerry, who lays hands on the sick, the deaf hear and the blind see, is now here to heal these blind children." My thoughts immediately said, "Thanks a whole lot, Bro! Wow! No pressure here to perform or anything!"

I had prayed for the blind and deaf before this event and experienced the miracle of healing. Yet, nothing had prepared me for this. It was a convergence of fear and faith, with fear winning by knockout. The "healer" felt sick to his stomach.

Some stories beg for a dramatic ending. My good friend, Sri Lankan National Leader and Co-Chair of the Foursquare Global Council Dr. Leslie Keegel, tells one. Unbeknownst to him, his overly eager assistants one day set up an impromptu "healing session" at a Buddhist house for the deaf and blind. They proceeded to tell Leslie that they had also promised this house that "all will be healed" — Nothing like pressure! As Leslie tells it humbly, all were healed.

Still fearful, I forced myself on, shouting loudly and overcompensating with anointing oil—as if either would force the hand of God.

I watched helplessly as the kids were loaded back on the bus, even before my message was delivered, all, to my knowledge, unhealed.

I've intentionally started this book with "my failure" in the Philippines. (If you are wondering…no, it wasn't my last one.) I do so because the story exemplifies the premise for everything I will write.

It's all about Him. His power. His glory. Just make sure you're in the position to see what He is doing and trust Him for the results. My emphasis throughout this book is to see from the scriptures how we must be positioned if we are to participate in His miracles.

I also want you to trust me on the stories I will share. Writing about the miraculous can raise suspicion, and rightfully so. Too many have exaggerated or told outright lies. God doesn't need our help. He wants our devotion based on honesty and truth.

Being "positioned" for miracles in your life is ultimately about a lifestyle. You can't turn it on and off. You must decide if you want to live a life that sees God do Kingdom of God, in the words of the late John Wimber, "stuff." You must desire to walk in faith, live a life pleasing to Him, and be willing to risk, even fail. There is no secret formula.

In fact, praying for healing and miracles can be hard work. You'll experience fear, discouragement, and even the contempt of fellow believers. It can get worse.

*L*iving a life that moves in the miraculous is not a private affair. It's not for the selfish or the loner.

Speaking of the late John Wimber, founder of the Vineyard churches and someone who experienced thousands of extraordinary miracles, he related that not only did the first hundred people he prayed for not get healed, but he often ended up with their sickness!

Still want to keep reading?

The Challenge

After speaking with hundreds of Christian leaders from around the world, I'm convinced that the United States is ripe for a renaissance in the miraculous. People from most every other religion known to man, even those we have often believed were "unreachable," are now encountering Jesus in powerful, supernatural ways, all over the world. God is pouring out His Spirit to win the lost in regions of the world many have given up on.

Unfortunately, some of us have given up on America. It's too secular or pagan. It's Godless, lawless, and in need of judgment. Maybe so, but where sin abounds, doesn't grace follow? The gifts of the Holy Spirit are available to the believer to touch a broken world. Isn't this what Jesus said He came for?

> *"The Spirit of the Lord is upon ME,*
> *Because HE anointed ME to preach the gospel to the poor.*
> *HE has sent ME to proclaim release to the captives,*
> *And recovery of sight to the blind,*

TO set free those who are oppressed,
TO proclaim the favorable year of the Lord."
Luke 4:18

Will not the Lord give these gifts to those who ask of Him and want to use them to further His Kingdom?

America needs to repent. Yes. Could not believers walking in love and in power help to bring that about? Living a life that moves in the miraculous is not a private affair. It's not for the selfish or the loner. To the contrary, it is for the blessing of others: our church, community, and even the world.

Finally, I'm a simple practitioner, not an advanced theologian; I do my best to practice what the Bible teaches. But I do consider myself a serious student of the Bible. That is why you'll read an equal amount of personal stories and scripture.

I take very seriously Paul's admonition to "handle accurately the word of truth." And I truly believe that the passages I've included will reach deeply into your soul and spirit. Prayerfully, my stories will only confirm that the Word is "living and active."

Enjoy the journey,

Jerry

Chapter 1

THE GREATEST MIRACLE

Many have asked, "What is the greatest miracle you've ever witnessed?" You might be surprised.

My son, Jeremiah, and I went to Tanna Island, Vanuatu, formerly known as the New Hebrides, to minister with our Foursquare leaders. For such a small geographical location, this is a place that has garnered a lot of attention in the past. It was the home of John and Mary Paton, the historic missionaries who arrived on Tanna, November 5, 1858. They built a small house and began trying to minister to the natives, many of whom were from the cannibalistic tribes spread throughout the area. This is the place Billy Graham writes about in his book *Angels*. Graham shares the story of the Patons and how angels protected them when tribesmen surrounded their

> What else he was about to share left me with the overwhelming realization that I was going to be a part of something historic, if not miraculous.

small home with the intent of killing them and, of course, having them for dinner.

We spent the night not far from the tiny airport, staying in a small bungalow that belonged to Chief Tom Numake who was our First Foursquare President of Vanuatu and the Vanuatu Chief of Chiefs at the time. Jeremiah got up early and immediately he found the son-in-law of Chief Tom. He had a small boat and was willing to take him fishing just off shore. They came back a few hours later with a couple of really nice Wahoo fish. It was a good thing he did, because those two fish and some rice ended up being our breakfast, lunch, and dinner for the next few days. Soon the big day arrived and we took a 4-wheel-drive to an even more remote part of the island.

Sitting on the top of a grassy knoll on a South Pacific island time had forgotten, I listened as the tribal leader, Isaac Wan, spoke. I watched in the corner of my eye as the small children ran wild, naked, only challenged by the many communal pigs and other animals that darted between the dozens of little huts built out of bamboo and grass.

The adults of this village wore their Sunday best, surprisingly westernized clothing. The air was still on a mild overcast day keeping the red, white, and blue flag limp. It held the honored position in this village—it was an American flag.

This leader and his village were all part of a cult, specifically a "cargo cult." Cargo cults were a phenomenon created primarily during World War II when cargo containers, meant for soldiers, were dropped inadvertently into primitive people groups. Villagers would discover the delicacies of what were called "C-Rations" at the time. Today they are called M.R.E.s or "Meals Ready to Eat." This particular cult worshiped everything they knew about America and a man whom they referred to as John Frum.

The origins of this man are sketchy at best. Some said his name was a variation of the phrase "John from America." John Frum was their "God, Jesus" according to Isaac Wan and his disciples (estimated at up to 20,000 devotees). They had been waiting a long time for his glorious return. They would have to keep waiting. But something much better, beyond any materialistic dreams, was about to happen.

Just the day before we had met, Isaac said that he was expecting me—waiting for an American pastor to come to his village. What else he was about to share left me with the overwhelming realization that I was going to be a part of something historic, if not miraculous. Knowing that something of huge magnitude is about to happen can slow time down and bring a flood of memories alive again.

Divine Intervention

When I was a small boy, my mother and father divorced. Before that time, I remember fighting, dishes flying, yelling, and rage. This filled me with so much depression and anxiety that I wanted to run away from home to escape it. I even tried to run away once, but like most young children, I turned back as soon as I realized that I had nowhere to sleep and no food to eat. It was during this tumultuous period that I first felt the presence of God in my life.

There was a small church just up the street from our house. I would watch every Sunday and Wednesday night as loads of kids would get out of their cars with their parents and go in to the church. They fascinated me because they always seemed to be happy to be there and they ran to their classrooms like it was the most exciting thing on earth. I seem to remember that most of the cars had a bumper sticker on them that read "I Found It," which had the desired effect of making me extremely curious as to what it was that they had found.

One day I asked my mother if I could go to that church the following Sunday. She agreed, but said, "You have to dress up really nice if you want to go to church." The next Sunday I was very excited about going to that place where everyone seemed to be happy. Almost as soon as I sat down in the Sunday school class, the teacher asked, "Is there anyone here who doesn't know Jesus and doesn't know if you will go to

> *I* knew then that truly my life was in God's hands. That single event, and God's intervention in it, again changed the course of my life.

Heaven?" I immediately raised my hand. The other kids laughed at me as if I had said something funny, or had tripped and fallen down or something, and I didn't understand at all why they were laughing.

After class, the Sunday school teacher zoomed right in on me. She took out a small cartoon character booklet about a boy close to my age who learned about the truth of the gospel. The teacher asked if I wanted what Jesus was offering to me and if I would invite Him into my heart and life. We prayed together and I said a simple prayer asking Jesus into my heart. At just seven years of age, I felt Him come in and immediately change my life. I began telling everyone I knew about what had happened to me.

Later, after my parents divorced, I was shuttled back and forth between my mother and stepfather, and my severely depressed and alcoholic father. We moved from one dilapidated rental to another, and I was forced to spend hours and hours in bars with my dad. In the midst of this, I could still see the Hand of God in my life. Statistically speaking, I could have easily turned to alcohol and/or drugs myself and ended up in the social welfare system or on the street, but God's staying power was with me.

Two of the Sunday school teachers from that church down the street took an interest in that poorly dressed little boy, and kept track of him no matter where he moved. They paid my way to all the church camps and special children's events, and treated me like their own family. One of them even gave me my first Bible. I still remember it clearly; it had a brown leather cover and had my name on the front in gold lettering. I was so proud of it that I kept it under my pillow at night.

That same dear saint even went out of her way to pick me up and take me to church every Sunday, no matter where I had moved, until eventually they revoked her driver's license for poor eyesight and advanced age. I am eternally grateful that God loved me so much that He sent those two dear ones to love and care for me. They were indeed a miracle to an undeserving boy who might not have otherwise stood a chance in life.

My teenage years gave God another opportunity to intervene in my life in a miraculous way. Before turning 16 years old, and before I even had my first driver's license, I began to save money to buy a car. I didn't have much, but everything I had went into buying a 1968 Buick Riviera. The car was huge, and probably had far too much motor for a 16-year-old who was all too eager to slam the pedal to the floor and burn up the tires.

One Saturday morning, I was on my way to work my normal weekend job. An older woman had hired me to do odd jobs on her large property and rentals, and as I was running late, I was driving every bit of the speed limit, and then some. In the opposite lane, screaming toward me came a large nineteen sixty-something Chevy Impala. There was another driver in front of me trying to turn. I realized that I was going too fast to stop, and I knew that within a split second we were going to crash. Suddenly I felt two large Hands press against my chest and throw me back tightly against the car seat. Back then, wearing a seatbelt was optional, and I was not wearing mine, but those Hands held me tightly against the seat. Both vehicles were completely totaled. I should have gone through the windshield, but I didn't even bump my head or chest on the dash or on the steering wheel. I walked away from the accident, but the driver and passenger of the other vehicle were rushed to the emergency room. I knew then that truly my life was in God's hands. That single event, and God's intervention in it, again changed the course of my life.

Back to Tanna

Isaac Wan, the cargo cult leader, told me that God had spoken to him and told him that he needed to "repent." This time the cult leader was being challenged "to repent" by none other than Jesus Christ.

Isaac, in his "negotiations" with Jesus, said he would repent when an American pastor would come. None had come until now.

So there I stood, obligatory white shirt and tie, looking my best to portray an American pastor. Chief Barnabas Tausi (Foursquare president of Vanuatu at the time) stood close to me, broad shouldered, wearing a colorful, tropical, short-sleeved shirt, ready to interpret my short evangelistic sermon, while my son, Jeremiah, stood by taking photos of this historic event.

The crowd waited patiently and Isaac wasted no time. He got on his knees and repented before God and man. He told his people that the cult was wrong and it was time for a change. As soon as he finished, I laid my hands on him and prayed, asking the Lord to now use him for His glory and purpose. He then handed me the megaphone to preach. Standing on the short hill, I felt a connection to Jesus standing on the mount teaching the Beatitudes to the people.

I did my best to preach a pure gospel message of salvation that only comes through Jesus Christ. I really didn't spend that much time. But when I paused, I gave an altar call, as I always do, for those who wanted to respond to salvation. To my absolute amazement, it appeared to be over ninety percent of those listening who flooded to the makeshift altar area below where I was speaking to them. I prayed with them. They lifted their hearts and lifted their hands and received Jesus Christ as their Savior. This great experience always reminds me that the greatest miracle of all is when someone gives their life to Jesus Christ. Nothing else is greater than that, because that is the time we enter into eternity with Him and Him alone.

Within six months of our trip to Vanuatu, Rev. Luke Franklin (Foursquare General Supervisor) reported back to me that they believed nearly 11,000 of the cargo cult followers had come to Christ. Isaak Tu (the son of Isaac

Wan) still pastors a Foursquare church in Tanna Island to this day. How privileged I am to have been **Positioned** for the **Miracle** of salvation to those precious souls on Tanna Island that historic day.

Through this life we do need miracles, and miracles come our way as a gift from the Savior. But the greatest miracle of all is always salvation through Jesus Christ. When someone is drawn to the Lord, hears the message of the gospel, then receives that gift of eternal life—there is no miracle on this earth, or in this lifetime, that can surpass that.

Where to Start: The 7 Ingredients

Jesus' first miracle was recorded at the wedding at Cana. Within this passage in John 2, I have discovered seven ingredients, or principles, that come from both scripture and personal experience, that are essential for the consistent appearance of the miraculous. Not every miracle requires all seven principles; sometimes it only takes one. But when more of these principles are operating consistently in your life, there is greater opportunity to see the miraculous.

My very life is a miracle. Jeremiah, the prophet, was told by God, "Before I formed you in the womb I knew you." (Jeremiah 1:5) This scripture resonates deeply with me because I am a living testimony to God's interest in the individual life. God preserved my life as a young boy and powerfully encouraged me as a young man. Seeing His hand laid the foundation for the miracles I experience today.

Think back…I'm sure you too recall how God has brought you to this very place in time, preparing you, positioning you to see clearly "that which the Father is doing."

Chapter 2

THE POSITION OF HUMILITY

Miracle Ingredient 1 of 7: Bring it to Him

I could see her desperation as she approached me. This attractive Fijian woman of Indian descent needed a miracle. In her culture, women who cannot conceive are devalued. Doctors told her it would be absolutely impossible for her to have a child. Making matters worse, her marriage was being adversely impacted.

She asked me to pray. Normally, after any service I would do so. But this time, I sensed the Holy Spirit telling me to wait until I could pray with her and her husband. She was broken and continued pleading, "Please Pastor, please, pray for me." As heartwrenching as this was, I knew I needed to be

I looked her in the eyes and said, "Thus says the Lord, you are completely healed. You will surely have the child in your arms by this time next year."

obedient. Finally, she invited me to come to her home the following day when her husband would be there.

That night I went to my room, excited about all the things the Lord had done during the night's meeting. When I closed the door behind me, I turned and was greeted by an unexpected visitor.

Like most developing nations, encounters with the supernatural are commonplace. Fiji, despite its association with island paradise, is no exception. Fijian history, dating back to the 19th century according to locals, was filled with various forms of sorcery and witchcraft. The Fijian witch held an infamous place in Fijian lore. She resembled the mythical Medusa with hair active, climbing upward as if her locks were snakes. Her translucent image hung in the air like a body floating in water.

The only problem was that my visitor fit the locals' description of the witch exactly, and she was very, very angry—at me. Though she made no sounds, her face filled with rage—her eyes black and piercing with hate and shifting in every direction independently.

I've encountered the demonic many times before, but never such an apparition. Still full of the Spirit, I leaned toward her as if to say, "You don't scare me!" and then shouted, "Well, I guess I made the devil mad!"

She disappeared instantly, but more evil was waiting for me the next day.

I really didn't know at the time why this thing had appeared to me, but the following day, when I arrived at the barren woman's house, I felt an evil presence again. I was looking for the woman's house number, not knowing whether hers was the house on the right or the left, and this sense of malevolence came at me from the house on the right. It made the hair stand up on the back of my neck. I paused and rebuked the evil presence and it left in an instant. My friend and I pressed on toward the door and, to my relief, the house we were to be visiting was the one on the left.

Upon entering, the first thing I asked the woman was, "Who lives next door?" She was surprised at the question but answered, "All those people there have idols everywhere in the house and serve all kinds of other gods."

In contrast, this woman's home was full of the presence of the Lord. Satan evidently was upset at what he knew could happen here, and how it could impact their community. Without wasting any more time, I told the woman and her husband to stand and hold hands, and that I would pray that they would have a baby soon. No sooner had I touched them when the woman fell to the ground under the power of the Holy Spirit. Her husband seemed taken back and didn't understand why she was lying on their small living room floor. But as I pulled her back to her feet, I did something I had only done similarly once before. I looked her in the eyes and said, "Thus says the Lord, you are completely healed. You will surely have the child in your arms by this time next year."

Thinking back on that makes me tremble, because it had to be the boldness of the Holy Spirit or I would have been in trouble! I believe now that it was what the Bible calls the *gift of faith* as described in I Corinthians 12:9. My friend and I then left this couple's home, not knowing if we would ever see them again.

Many times when I pray for people I never hear the results or get to know what God did for someone after I'm gone. In this case, however, God was gracious and gave me a glimpse of His awesome power.

One year later, my wife, Julie, and I were in that same area preaching at another service. When I was about to share my message for the evening, a woman came running up to me holding a baby and shouting, "Pastor Jerry, Pastor Jerry, look!" I did not recognize her, and being polite I said, "Yes, that's nice, you have a beautiful baby." She said again, "Pastor Jerry, look!" She must have known from my expression that I had forgotten who she was, because she went on to refresh my memory of the visit to her house the year before. She then explained to me that within one week of our prayer for her she had become pregnant. She said, "It's a miracle, the Lord has healed me!"

Some ten years later, my good friend, Satish, met me in Fiji when I was visiting that area again. He reminded me about that day when we had prayed together for that dear woman and her husband. He told me that this incredible story had spread throughout the entire town and had caused them to believe in the God who cares for our every need if we but bring it to Him.

The 1st Ingredient: Bring it to Him

The turning of water into wine was Jesus' first recorded miracle. For various reasons, believers have struggled with this action. To some it seems too practical—beneath the Lord of the universe. It smacks of magic, a slight of hand, a parlor trick. Yet, within this miracle is a kind of template of what ingredients are needed to see divine intervention. Maybe Jesus' first miracle was intentionally pragmatic to help us mere mortals see that we too can play, not just as spectators, and that not all miracles need a Charlton Heston, Hollywood style parting of the waters.

There was a first ingredient to changing the water into wine. It was exercised by the barren woman in Fiji—bring it to Jesus. No matter what the issue or need, Jesus is willing to be involved. Some may think that goes without saying, but I've found, unfortunately, it is the most common mistake of even faithful believers. We think of going to Jesus as a last resort, not a first action. Without this principle as a foundation in your faith walk, your opportunities to see the miraculous will diminish.

Your position must be one of humility. The humble believer looks first to their Savior. If that smacks of "Old

Time Religion," well, maybe there are some things we should go back to.

> *On the third day there was a wedding in Cana of Galilee, and the mother of Jesus was there; and both Jesus and His disciples were invited to the wedding. When the wine ran out, the mother of Jesus said to Him, "They have no wine." And Jesus said to her, "Woman, what does that have to do with us? My hour has not yet come." John 2:1-4*

When I first read this passage, it seemed to me that Jesus was acting almost rudely and disrespectfully toward His mother, which I know is opposed to His character. So I dug deeper to find out why. I noticed that Mary didn't get offended at being talked to in this manner; she simply ignored His statement and went ahead and asked the servants to fill the jars with water. She assumed He would go ahead and do the miracle she requested, in spite of His voiced objections to the timing of it, and He honored her faith in this matter. I also wondered why Mary bothered. It doesn't seem like this was that big of a deal anyway. It was, at worst, a matter of a little embarrassment that the wedding planners

> *Jesus will always be the answer to whatever your problem is, no matter how great or how small.*

hadn't planned well enough. Why was it so important to her that He do this? Then it hit me between the eyes: There is no issue we have in our lives that God is not interested in, and Mary knew this principle. This seems an insignificant problem for the King of Kings and Lord of Lords to give His attention to, but He did it anyway.

He is never too uncaring, too busy, overworked, or so preoccupied with running the universe that He won't take notice of even the smallest things in our lives, if we ask Him to. We see over and over in the Bible that at times Jesus unexpectedly invaded people's lives, such as with Zachaeus and the lame man at the pool of Bethesda. At other times we see Him waiting to be invited into the situation, as in the case of the blind man on the road to Jericho and the disciples on the road to Emmaus. To default to an attitude of "If it's God's will …" definitely results in seeing less miracles.

No matter what the issue or need, Jesus is willing to be involved. The first step is always to recognize His desire to work with us by inviting Him to do so. Matthew 7:7-8 says:

> *Ask, and it will be given to you; seek, and you will find; knock, and it will be opened to you. For everyone who asks receives, and he who seeks finds, and to him who knocks it will be opened.*

Jesus will always be the answer to whatever your problem is, no matter how great or how small. I can't stress enough how very important it is to get your problem to Him.

When Jesus answered Mary's request at the wedding at Cana, He said, "Woman, what does that have to do with us? My hour has not yet come." Some translate this as, "Who has related this to Me?" or "Why do you involve me in this?" or "Who has brought Me into this situation?" It is my experience that the people who get answers are the people who bring Jesus into the situation. Mary knew that her miracle could only come when Jesus became involved in her need.

Another story illustrating this principle is found in Matthew:

> *A Canaanite woman from that region came out and began to cry out, saying, "Have mercy on me, Lord, Son of David; my daughter is cruelly demon-possessed." But He did not answer her a word. And His disciples came and implored Him, saying, "Send her away, because she keeps shouting at us." But He answered and said, "I was sent only to the lost sheep of the house of Israel." But she came and began to bow down before Him, saying, "Lord, help me!" And He answered and said, "It is not good to take the children's bread and throw it to the dogs." But she said, "Yes, Lord; but even the dogs feed on the crumbs which fall from their masters' table." Then Jesus said to her, "O woman, your faith is great; it shall be done for you as you wish."*
> *Matthew 15:22-28*

The Position of Humility

I think most people would agree that, at first glance, Jesus seemed to treat this woman very rudely. The first time I read this story, I was a little shocked that He essentially called her a dog. She was not a Jew, and there were definitely cultural attitudes in place which would have explained a normal Jew calling a Canaanite a dog, but Jesus wasn't a normal Jew. His disciples acted in character of the norm by asking Jesus to get rid of her because she was being annoying. But Jesus is always kind, isn't He? Actually, there are many instances where Jesus seems to be "testing the mettle" of an individual. He wanted to know how she would react: faith or fear, pride or humility. Another thing to note is that this woman approached Jesus using a pious Jewish saying, "Thou son of David." Perhaps she thought that the right religious words and identification with the right religious group would carry some weight with Jesus. It didn't. Jesus' initial response may have been a reaction to her false religious approach.

Her response was amazing. She didn't get offended. She had a one-track mission to see her daughter delivered, and she didn't care what she was called. She believed that He was the only One who could provide her miracle, and she was

> *He* is the only One who can meet our need and provide our miracle, but also we have to come with humility and confidence.

determined to get it. Finally, she dropped the religious cloak and simply said, "Lord, help me!" That was all He needed to hear, and she got her miracle, and a mention in the annals of history as being a woman of great faith.

This is a pivotal principle when we come to Jesus. Not only do we have to recognize that He is the only One who can meet our need and provide our miracle, but also we have to come with humility and confidence. We must have the attitude that no one can talk us out of it or trigger a pride response that might make us back off from getting what we need.

Believe me; Jesus will test us on this. How many times have we suffered through something because we thought we were too unimportant or not good enough to bring our small (or great) need to Jesus? Or the opposite, that it was too embarrassing to humble ourselves to ask someone to pray for us or to go forward in church in front of everyone in order to receive the prayer that might lead to us receiving what we need? How much do we really want it? Do we want it enough to be persistent? Do we want it enough to humble ourselves? Because that determination is what it takes.

Born Without Eardrums

At our church in Southern California, we had gone through about a six-month period in which we were experiencing a wave of incredible healings and miracles.

One night, many people gathered for a service specifically set aside for healing. The whole purpose of the meeting was to have people come themselves, and bring their friends and family, their co-workers, and their neighbors to the church to be anointed with oil and prayed for.

Our services always began with praise and worship so that we could draw near to the presence of the Lord. When conducting healing services in any location, it was my habit to always ask the sick to come to the front of the room. I wanted to see those who were in need as well as to be close enough to discern where the presence of the Lord was moving. Often I would not even wait until the worship service was over, but would walk around and begin to pray for people as I felt led to do so by the Holy Spirit.

During these services, parents would often bring their children who had various sicknesses and ailments. During one of these services, two different sets of parents each brought a child born without eardrums. As I was walking around and praying, I began to lay hands on the people that I felt God wanted me to touch. I came to a young girl that I guessed was 11-13 years old. I laid my hands on her, not knowing what was wrong with her or why her parents had brought her. She immediately began to scream. It almost scared me to death! I thought that perhaps a demon or some mental illness was manifesting itself. Her parents immediately took her out of the service to try to calm her down. Later, the parents came back inside with tears running down their faces. I asked if they were okay, and they told me that the reason their daughter had been screaming was that she had been deaf and could suddenly hear. The praise and worship was so loud and so strange to her that it had frightened her and she began to scream. This brought tears to my eyes and we were all crying together. It impacted me so much that I will never forget that day.

That same night, a 19-year-old young man was brought to me for prayer. His hearing was instantly healed as well, but the miracle didn't stop there. He immediately began to speak in other tongues. He was not only healed, but filled with the Spirit. The following week, the same people brought him back to be prayed for again. When I asked why and was he okay, they said that he was fine, but that he prayed in tongues night and day. They wanted prayer for him to shut up. Needless to say, this was one prayer request I absolutely refused to pray for!

Remember: A miracle is something that does not happen naturally. It is something that only God can do, and only God can take credit for. If there is something that you need, and I mean *really* need, and you have no way to get it for yourself, and no one else can give it to you, then that is the time we have no choice except to live without it or bring it to Jesus. Why not bring your need to Him?

Chapter 3

THE POSITION OF OBEDIENCE

Miracle Ingredient 2 of 7: Do as He Says

I watched the white cane sliding side to side, like a divining rod coming toward me. Its owner was a middle-aged man whose blank stare only confirmed the obvious: He was totally blind.

Our church here in the States had been experiencing healings on a regular basis. But this was the first blind person to enter our doors. I would encounter many more in later ministry, but this was the first time, and I wasn't prepared. My heart sank. Fear was slugging it out with faith. If this was a ten round prize fight, my faith staggered for the first four.

My mind raced through passages in the Bible that involved the blind. The one I focused on was where Jesus

Have you ever prayed a prayer that you didn't want to end, because then you'd have to open your eyes and face a harsh reality?

spit in the dirt and applied mud to the blind man's eyes. A bottle of mud in the room would have been nice. I did have anointing oil, so I put it over his eyes and prayed.

Have you ever prayed a prayer that you didn't want to end, because then you'd have to open your eyes and face a harsh reality? But when my prayer ended, something extraordinary happened. The blind man fell to the floor. *A good time to turn and pray for others*, I thought. Maybe the crowd wouldn't notice if the blind man was healed or not.

"I still can't see! I still can't see!" the still blind man yelled in a panic, foiling my ecclesiastical bait and switch.

Thank God for help. The blind man's friend intervened. "You can't see because you refuse to give your life to Jesus," he said. I finally exhaled.

"I will if you tell me how," the blind man said and turned to me. Leading people in the sinner's prayer was something I could do. We finished praying out loud together "…In Jesus' name, amen!"

The blind man's blank stare slowly faded to a focus on the faces of the people around him. His friend asked, "Can you see?" He then held up one finger, then two, then three. The blind man, no longer sightless, counted them out correctly. He regained his full sight, joining the congregation in jumping and shouting with joy.

And it all started with simple obedience.

The 2nd Ingredient: Do as He Says

His mother said to the servants, "Whatever He says to you, do it." John 2:5

It is human nature to come to God when we have a problem, are sick, or are in a difficulty in which there seems no way out. People turn to God in moments when they have tried everything else and none of it has worked. God is gracious and still responds to these needs; but often those who receive from Him don't have a relationship with Him or walk away from Him even after He answers their request. I have heard that people say, "Lord, I went to church on Easter and Christmas, and put $5 in the offering basket. Why aren't you answering my prayer?" People want something from Him when they are in need, but haven't a clue about serving Him out of love and relationship. His promises are usually tied to obedience to Him, while in relationship with Him. "If…then …" is a common paradigm of the Old Testament, beginning in Genesis. He created Adam and Eve to literally walk and talk with Him daily. This was His intention for all

> *But those who see consistent miracles in their lives, on a daily basis, are those who walk with Him on a daily basis. It only makes sense!*

men (and women) but rebellion and disobedience made that impossible.

> *They heard the sound of the Lord God walking in the garden in the cool of the day and the man and his wife hid themselves from the presence of the Lord God among the trees of the garden. Then the Lord God called to the man, and said to him, "Where are you?" Genesis 3:8-9*

Adam and Eve had a very close walk with Him before the fall, but felt they had to hide themselves after. Guilt always gets in the way of intimacy. Once they had disobeyed God, He had to ask them where they were because they were hiding themselves from the presence of the Lord. In the New Testament, John said,

> *Beloved, if our heart does not condemn us, we have confidence before God, and whatever we ask we receive from Him, because we keep His commandments and do the things that are pleasing in His sight. 1 John 3:21-22*

This is such a good illustration of why we need to keep our consciences clean and stay in close relationship with Him. While we are walking in this close relationship with God, we can expect Him to take care of us and give us those things that we need and even want.

Some people take this out of context and expect that God is Santa Claus, who has to give us whatever is "on our list" because we asked Him. But if you read this verse carefully, you see that we have to have a clear conscience (our heart does not condemn us), obey Him (keep His commandments), and walk in a love relationship with Him at all times (do the things that are pleasing in His sight). What I mean is that beyond even the obvious Ten Commandments, we seek a life that is spent to listen and live according to every word Jesus spoke and the lifestyle He demonstrated.

> *...He gives the Spirit without measure. The Father loves the Son and has given all things into His hand. He who believes in the Son has eternal life; but he who does not obey the Son will not see life, but the wrath of God abides on him.*
> *John 3:34-36*

When it comes to miracles, God will reach the lost without these prerequisites in order to show Himself real to them and draw them in. But with His family, we need to have faith. We can't have faith to see Him perform these miracles if we aren't meeting the above conditions. Faith requires confidence in Him, and if we don't have a clear conscience, we can't have that confidence.

This isn't a guilt trip, but rather an exhortation to stay close to Jesus and walk with Him "in the garden, in the cool of the day."

This is a theme throughout the Bible:

> *(Enoch) walked with God; and he was not, for God took Him. Genesis 5:22-24*

He was 365 years old, and never had to die, because he was so close to God!

> *(Noah) was a righteous man, blameless in his time; and he walked with God. Genesis 6:9*

Throughout scripture, it seems clear that those who loved God and were even passionate about Him were the ones who saw God opening the most doors for them. I don't mean to imply that we "earn" from Him answers to our prayers, because this is not the case. He meets us all where we are. But those who see consistent miracles in their lives, on a daily basis, are those who walk with Him on a daily basis. It only makes sense!

Abraham is a great example of this. He wasn't always perfect, but he was willing to obey God and follow whatever God asked him to do, including leaving his homeland and spending most of his life "on the road," as it were, camping out in tents. Because of his great faith and obedience, God said to Abraham:

> *Indeed, I will greatly bless you, and I will greatly multiply your seed as the stars of the heavens, and as the sand which is on the seashore; and your seed shall possess the gate of their enemies. And in your seed all the nations of the earth shall be blessed, because you have obeyed My voice." Genesis 22:17-18*

Moses, too, is a prime example of the correlation between closeness with God and seeing consistent miracles in a life. After him, we have the example of Joshua. Exodus 33:11 says:

> *Thus the Lord used to speak to Moses face to face, just as a man speaks to his friend. When Moses returned to the camp, his servant Joshua, the son of Nun, a young man, would not depart from the tent.*

Moses was so close to God that he walked with Him face to face. Joshua was so hungry for the presence of God that he would linger in the tent after Moses left just to soak it up.

I believe strongly that if we had that kind of hunger for the touch of God, we would experience His intervention at every step of our lives. God seems to always do amazing miracles with those who keep themselves close to Him.

The Jingling Keys

One year, while I was pastoring a church in Southern California, I was preparing to go to Vietnam to train other pastors and Bible school students. I was scheduled to speak there for five full 8-10 hour days as well as at some Sunday services. Before leaving on my trip, I gave a sermon in my church about what a great example Jesus is of being the ultimate servant. My text was from Philippians 2:3-11:

> *Do nothing from selfishness or empty conceit, but with humility of mind regard one another as more important than yourselves; do not merely look out for your own personal interests, but also for the interests of others. Have this attitude in yourselves which was also in Christ Jesus, who, although He existed in the form of God, did not regard equality with God a thing to be grasped, but emptied Himself, taking the form of a bond-servant, and being made in the likeness of men. Being found in appearance as a man, He humbled Himself by becoming obedient to the point of death, even death on a cross. For this reason also, God highly exalted Him, and bestowed on Him the name which is above every name, so that at the name of Jesus every knee will bow, of those who are in heaven and on earth and under the earth, and that every tongue will confess that Jesus Christ is Lord, to the glory of God the Father.*

As I was teaching on those verses, I became very passionate about this message. I was running a little overtime (as usual), but felt very strongly that the church needed to hear this teaching and apply it to their lives.

While I was waxing passionately eloquent, a woman seated right next to the center aisle pulled out her car keys and began jingling them. She immediately distracted my train of thought and got my attention. When my eyes were clearly fixed on her, she turned her head and looked back at the clock on the back wall. This was obviously meant to remind me that I was running over time.

This really ticked me off. I knew exactly what was on her mind: She wanted to get to the restaurant before noon so that she could beat the after-church Sunday rush.

> *I decided then and there that I would rather extend whatever gifts I had to hungry people who want Jesus, rather than placating those who are more interested in the food on their plates.*

I took her hint and closed the service with an altar call. I felt very disappointed and let down because I had felt such an unction to bring this message, and imagined a much greater response. I have seen tremendous altar calls, with people cramming to the front to commit their lives to Christ or to follow Him more fully—but not this time. This time, only two people came forward to commit to being more of a servant to Christ and His church. I was so disappointed that I didn't want to talk to anyone after the service.

Later that evening, as I was boarding my flight to Vietnam, the leaders gave me a huge list of the teachings that they wanted me to bring during the week that I was there.

As I perused the list, I saw that Philippians 2 was on it. My heart fell. I did not want to preach that sermon, because it obviously was one of my worst. My church back home seemed completely unmoved by it, and were more interested in beating the after-church lunch crowd than in listening to my obviously boring sermon.

After arriving in Vietnam, I hit the ground running. They immediately put me on the back of a small motorbike, but not before putting a long-sleeved shirt on me, and a hat, and sunglasses so that I would not stand out to everyone as a Westerner. They took me down back roads and alleys to eventually arrive at the secret Bible school.

They had placed my speaking time slot—you guessed it—right before lunch! I was sure they would be thinking more about their upcoming meal than my boring sermon, so I hurried through the materials at lightning speed and planned to give no room at all for an altar call.

To my amazement, halfway through rattling off my materials, one of the students threw himself prostrate on the concrete floor and began crying out, "Oh God, forgive me that I'm not a servant like Jesus."

Soon everyone in the room followed the example of this very passionate young man. Since they were all on the ground facing me, I had no choice but to back against the wall, sit, and wait while these amazing students cried out to God for what must have been over an hour.

This was in stark contrast to people who cared more for their noon-day lunch than for eternal truth.

As I looked around, I realized that this was no show of false humility designed to impress the teacher. There were pools of tears forming on the ground under each one of their faces. I was not even able to finish my message!

This was definitely a great defining moment in my life. I decided then and there that I would rather extend whatever gifts I had to hungry people who want Jesus, rather than placating those who are more interested in the food on their plates.

During that same week, one of the students came and talked to me after class. I really enjoy telling the stories of all the miracles I have seen, because we in the West are not used to seeing them and are amazed when we do. But this student said, "Pastor Jerry, you don't need to tell so many of those miracle stories. We like them, but we experience miracles every day. What we don't have is Bible teachers like yourself that will come and teach us the Word of God. So please just teach us the Bible. This is what we are the most desperate for."

With this kind of passion for relationship with Jesus, it is no wonder that these people experience miracles as a part of their everyday life.

"To obey is better than sacrifice." (1 Samuel 15:22) Miracles happen in the context of relationship. Relationships stay healthy when we obey the laws of love and fidelity. Do what He says…out of love hopefully; but, nevertheless, be obedient.

Chapter 4

THE POSITION OF GIVING

Miracle Ingredient 3 of 7: Give Him What You Have

One Sunday afternoon, I had just finished our last service and was very anxious to get home. As a family, we were getting ready to leave on our annual vacation. Hallelujah! We had almost three weeks away for some travel and to attend a family wedding on the east coast of the USA. I was tired and way overdue for some time away with the family.

Just as I was headed toward my car in the church parking lot, one of the parishioners came screeching to a stop in front of me. They said, "Pastor Jerry, please come to the hospital immediately." Apparently, the brother of one of our dearest church members was near death. He had actually been found dead but the paramedics were able to get

> *They pleaded with me to go in and do whatever I could to believe for a miracle of healing for this man who was so near to death.*

a weak heartbeat and get him on life-support. Once at the hospital he had suffered some complications and he was barely hanging on. Without hesitation I jumped into the car, called Julie to explain that I would be held up for a while, and then headed toward the local hospital.

When I arrived, I found our dear parishioner along with an absolutely packed-out hospital waiting room. All were part of his family and had rushed over after receiving the news from the doctor that his brother probably wouldn't make it. I was told that he was barely alive and that without the hospital equipment and life support, he would be gone for sure.

What broke my heart was that the man was a young father with a wife and small children to leave behind. His wife was crying as the doctor had just given her the grim news. This man's mother and father were in the waiting room as well. Everyone was absolutely crushed under the weight of this terrible news about their loved one.

Then the pressure began to hit me. I thought about this and wondered what I could really do to help in this dire situation. I was already too tired from the normal ministry load and really just wanted to get going on my vacation, free from the office, so to speak. However, I saw the weight of this horrific news that was absolutely sucking the life out of this precious family, and I knew I had to help if I could. My immediate thought was that most likely it was too late. The doctor's prognosis seemed sure, and they were confident enough of it that they asked all the family members to come and share their final goodbyes.

My initial thoughts were to just go in and say a nice quick prayer and then pray and comfort the family for what would most likely be an inevitable time of loss. I wanted to do my best just to let them know I cared, even though I knew I wouldn't be able to be there for the typical family care and perhaps funeral services that I might get invited to help with.

The interesting thing was that out of these many family members that were there at the hospital only one attended our church. I was not at all sure what kind of faith they themselves had for a miracle to take place. I of course remembered that the very thing that even stopped Jesus was the lack of faith among the people in His hometown:

> *And He could do no miracle there except that He laid His hands on a few sick people and healed them. Mark 6:5*

But, to my amazement, they still asked me to pray. They pleaded with me to go in and do whatever I could to believe for a miracle of healing for this man who was so near to death.

That particular Sunday I just happened to be in my very best suit that a church member had paid big time for, so on the outside I looked fairly together, if I do say so myself. I decided that I would bypass all the hospital procedures and just head right into the emergency care room without getting the clearance from the hospital staff. It seemed that the hospital staff must have thought I was somebody fairly official by their reaction everywhere I went. No one questioned who I was, where I was going, or who I was there to see. I was acknowledged everywhere with a "Good afternoon, sir!"

I proceeded through the hallways until I found our dear church member's brother. All the life support machines were up and running and I was almost afraid I would bump something and mess it up. My thoughts were to just pray a quick prayer that the man would hopefully make Heaven and that the family would survive and be comforted with the loss of this young father.

I proceeded to pray my quick, sincere prayer and believe for the best. Then something happened that was completely unexpected. All of a sudden, in the middle of my nice prayer, I heard the audible voice of God saying, "I will raise him on the third day."

My prayer stopped immediately because I had heard that voice twice before, and after both times I had notable breakthroughs and divine direction for my life. I stopped and said, "Lord, that sounded like you." The problem was that it sounded a bit too religious. "I will raise him on the third day."

I thought about it and figured I couldn't tell those hurting people a silly word like that and then get on a plane

The Position of Giving

when this man was about to die. How inconsiderate and cruel would it be for me to go to that poor hurting wife who was just told by the doctor that her husband would be gone soon, and tell her I had prayed and God said He "will raise him on the third day"? How ridiculous, I thought, especially when the doctors expect him to die now. What if that happens after I give this crazy word from God?

I also thought at that moment that I had finally gotten a good reputation in that city as a good, stable, and well-rounded pastor who was committed to the community. I had stayed longer than many others who had pastored there before me. I had community leaders in the church. We were known all over because of our food and clothing ministry as well as other outreach services to the community. I was also a police chaplain with city, state, and national awards for serving the police department and the community.

Now if I was to share this prophetic word with this hurting wife and mother and he died anyway I would be laughed at and considered a crazy, false prophet. This really put me in a tough dilemma. I wanted to stand in faith with these people, but also cared a whole lot about my good reputation.

With that, I knew I needed to pray and get more clarity from the Lord. I began talking to the ceiling and asking God if this bizarre and outlandish word was really from Him? By then the hospital staff had started staring in through the glass at me, wondering who was on the ceiling that I was talking to. I continued praying—talking to the Lord on the ceiling—and then said, "Lord, that really sounded like your voice to me, but before I can tell these hurting people such a word, I need a sign from you."

Thinking I could actually out-maneuver the Lord I said, "Lord, if that word was from you, and you want me to tell this family this and give them this hope, then open this man's eyes right now!" At the same time as I said "open this man's eyes," I pointed at his eyes, my hand just inches away from his face. To my unimaginable amazement, the guy opened his eyes. WOW! It scared me and humbled me at the same time. I thought and said, "Lord, that was a pretty good sign." But I did second-guess it and wondered if perhaps his body reactions just did that and it was just purely coincidental.

However, I rose up in faith and made up my mind to give this wonderful word about the healing of this man through the power of the Holy Spirit. Without hesitation, I went out and told this dying man's wife and family these words. I told them not to let the doctors take him off of life support, but continue to pray, for the Lord had said, "I will raise him on the third day," and he will be fine.

> *He* always takes into account our resources and our weaknesses, and often makes up for our lack.

We left the hospital to what would be the most unrestful vacation I have ever had. The whole time away I kept calling back home to check on the situation of this dying man. It seemed no one had heard anything at all, and hadn't seen or heard from the church member who asked me to pray for his brother in the first place. I thought to myself several times, "It's because he died." I figured he had probably died that day and the family was busy taking care of funeral proceedings and other family needs.

I knew my life and reputation in my church and community was now ruined. I continued in my self-absorbed vacation until it was time to come home and face the music. We arrived back on a Saturday, just in time for me to walk right in on the Sunday services. Before the first service, I began asking different people if they had heard anything about this or had seen the dear brother from our church. No one had heard a thing. I was sure that it was because his brother had died. I just knew that this man would probably never come back to be in a church with a pastor like me who had given him and his family such a false and cruel hope in their heartbreaking situation.

The worship service was just finishing and I grabbed the cordless microphone and was heading up to give my sermon, when our dear church member came in and said, "I have a testimony." He looked happy so I figured it must be good news. And it was. With that, I brought him up to the platform and he told the amazing results.

"All of you know what happened to my brother. Well, Pastor Jerry came and prayed and then told us, 'The Lord says he will rise on the third day.' He then told us to leave him on the life support. We listened, and on the third day my brother sat up and was completely healed. He even told us immediately that he needed to start going to church."

The amazing thing was that this man, who was so close to death, did begin coming to our church with his family. Actually, on our very last Sunday before deploying to the mission field, they were the last family to come hug us and say their goodbyes. He thanked me for praying for him that day and said that because of it his children still had a father and his wife still had a husband.

The 3rd Ingredient: Give Him What You Have

It is so easy to come up with excuses as to why we don't do what we should do, or why we don't see the results we want. We even have excuses as to why we won't come up to the front of a church and ask for prayer. We need to remember that God takes us where we are. Sometimes He asks something of us, and sometimes He doesn't; but He always takes into account our resources and our weaknesses, and often makes up for our lack.

This principle is found in 2 Corinthians 8:12. Paul tells the believers in Corinth:

> *For if the readiness is present, it is acceptable according to what a person has, not according to what he does not have.*

While Paul was specifically speaking about the giving of finances, genuine spiritual principles apply to every area of our lives as we walk with the Lord.

I have found that it takes humility to stand before Him and say, "It's just me, Lord! What you see is what you get. Do what you want with me." That is the kind of attitude God looks for, and when we have it, He will take those resources and multiply them into a miracle meant to be shared.

> *Now there were six stone waterpots set there for the Jewish custom of purification, containing twenty or thirty gallons each. Jesus said to them, "Fill the waterpots with water." And they filled them up to the brim. John 2:6-7*

God only asks for what we have, not for what we don't have. When He called Moses to deliver the children of Israel from the hands of their Egyptian oppressors, Moses felt absolutely powerless and insignificant for such a task. God knew how he felt, but said to him, "What is in your hand?" and Moses answered, "A staff." (Exodus 4:2)

The Bible doesn't say how Moses got the staff or how long he'd been walking around with it. It could have been something he picked up out in the wilderness while he was a shepherd for Jethro; no one knows. At any rate, it was of

> **Well, if I wasn't embarrassed already, it was about to get worse.**

little value, just an insignificant staff. But when it was given to God, it became an instrument that helped bring about the deliverance of millions of Israelites from the bondage of Egyptian slavery.

Jesus always did so much with so little. In Mark chapter 6, He fed 5,000 people, and in Mark chapter 8, He fed 4,000 with only a few loaves of bread and a few fish. People gave what they had, and Jesus, true to His God-nature, made it more than enough. A few vessels of water were enough to supply an entire wedding with the best wine. The widow's mite was enough to please the King of Kings. A handful of meal and a little oil given to the prophet turned into the salvation of the widow and her son. Take stock of what you have and give it to God, because He will use it, multiply it, and make you a blessing to the world with it.

Ministering Healing Even When I Was Sick

I had just finished three morning services and had gone to lunch with a few friends. We were eating sushi and having a good time when I tried a piece that I hadn't tried before. It was just a small piece on a variety plate of mixed sushi. It was so small that I basically just swallowed it whole. It was already down when I realized it was bad, but by then it was too late. Just after lunch, a businessman friend called and asked if I would come over and pray for his wife. I agreed and he came and picked me up about an hour or so later.

While driving to his house we hit some really heavy traffic. That's when it hit me. My stomach started to rumble and roar and rumble again. I said to myself, "Oh no, not now." With no place to stop, I was squirming all over the seat of my friend's Mercedes Benz, hoping and praying I wouldn't embarrass myself all over his beautiful car.

Finally, to my great relief, we made it to the house. My friend called his wife down to greet me at the bottom of the stairs. I said, "Hello, glad to be here to pray with you. Oh, can I first use your bathroom?" She directed me to the closest one and I shuffled myself in as fast as I could without having an accident. This has to have been the closest call I have ever had. Inside that bathroom I felt I died a thousand times. I was sitting and then kneeling, then sitting and then kneeling again. I'm sure you get the picture. After I had absolutely nothing left in me I finally tried to clean up, wipe the pouring sweat off of my face, and pull myself together enough to go out and pray for this poor woman who had just received the horrific news that she had cancer.

I had no doubt they had figured out why I was in there so long. I think it was at least 15-20 minutes of absolute agony. Well, if I wasn't embarrassed already, it was about to get worse. As soon as I walked out of the bathroom, my friend's primary school-aged daughter started to walk in. I put my hands up and told her she should not go in there now. She ignored me and went on in anyway. Within seconds, she came walking right back out holding her nose. She marched herself right up to me, still holding her nose, pointed her finger at me and shook her head. She then went to her dad, pulled on his shirt sleeve, pointed at me, and shook her head again while holding her nose.

I was terribly embarrassed, but there was nothing I could do about it. I had to decide if I should just ask my friend to take me back, or stay and give my all to pray for his dear wife. They would obviously understand if I left without praying. I knew I didn't have anything in me to give. But I also knew that God in his Word commanded:

> *Is anyone among you sick? Then he must call for the elders of the church and they are to pray over him, anointing him with oil in the name of the Lord; and the prayer offered in faith will restore the one who is sick, and the Lord will raise him up. James 5:14-15b*

I decided to stay and pray. I went ahead and put my hands on her head, as I have done with others thousands and thousands of times before, and prayed the best that I could under the circumstances.

After doing my best to pray and believe, I then asked my friend to take me back. For the next week I continued to be unimaginably sick and miserable. It was really awful because I had a long overseas flight in the middle of it.

Now the good news is that despite my severe weakness, my friend decided to take his wife to the doctor again for another checkup. He put his wife on a flight and went to one of the best hospitals in the region. The doctor checked and checked again and my friend's wife was able to fly home with the absolute joy that the cancer had completely left her body. I was finally feeling a bit better, and this news made *my* healing complete as well. This incredible healing proved to me how much we need to trust God, even when we might feel we have nothing to offer.

We often forget that it is not about how we feel or how strong we think we are in ourselves. We have to remember always that it is His power at work in us.

> *But we have this treasure in earthen vessels, so that the surpassing greatness of the power will be of God and not from ourselves. 2 Corinthians 4:7*

Chapter 5

THE POSITION OF RECEIVING

Miracle Ingredient 4 of 7: Keep Full of the Word and Spirit

"You're blowing it bro, stop it!"

That was from a friend who struggled to stay in his seat, gyrating from laughter as I spoke. I kept on, determined to at least finish my message. Hands continued to shake, sweat flowed, and words mumbled out barely coherent. No eye contact whatsoever. I didn't want to see what I could hear: Everyone laughing…laughing at me.

My very first sermon given in Bible college as a student was mercifully over. The teacher wasted no time calling me to the side and telling me to consider another profession—anything but preaching.

But I thought I had heard from God. I studied the Word. I prayed fervently. What would I do if not pastor? I never wanted to pastor a big church. My prayer was, "God, just give me 25 people I can

> *B*eing involved in the miraculous is the process of pouring out and being refilled.

love and teach about you, anywhere, in any small town in America where You would like me to go."

Obviously I had missed God. I would at least finish the semester then drop out. That night I cried out to God with all my heart. I told Him I loved Him and wanted to serve Him, but understood that He could never use someone so unable to speak, like me.

That same night a prophet/evangelist was scheduled to speak at a big youth event. He had a reputation of being extremely accurate with both the Word and prophetic words. Humiliated and depressed, I forced myself to go—coming in late, sitting in the back, hoping no fellow students would see me.

The preacher got up to share his message, but as soon as he had begun to preach he stopped suddenly and said, "I'm sorry I have to stop the message, but there is a young man in the service that the Lord has told me He wants to speak to." With that, he stepped off the platform, walked down the aisle, and began to look to the right and to the left of the audience, and then directly in my direction. When I saw him looking at me, and then walking toward me, I was scared to death. I was already sure that this had to be the

> We often need to push through the physical weariness and emotional drain brought on by the spiritual battle around us.

worst day of my life. Not only could I not preach or fulfill what I had thought was a call on my life, but now, I was certain that this prophet was going to tell all my fellow Bible school students and everyone else in the room what a terrible person I was.

He walked right up to my seat, pointed his finger at me and said, "You! God has a word for you today!" He then began to repeat word-for-word what I had spoken to God in my bedroom, and then went on to say that God had truly called me and had His hand on me, and he assured me that God had set me aside for His work. He went on to say that not only had I been called to do a work for the Lord, but that I would work with thousands and thousands of pastors and would see many nations open up before me.

Because he had spoken so accurately about the contents of my prayer to God which I had prayed alone in my bedroom, I believed the rest of his prophecy. At that moment, I knew for certain that God really did love me and was steering the course of my life.

> *Jesus said to them, "Fill the waterpots with water." So they filled them up to the brim. And He said to them, "Draw some out now and take it to the headwaiter." So they took it to him. When the headwaiter tasted the water which had become wine, and did not know where it came from (but the servants who had drawn the water knew), the headwaiter called the bridegroom, and said to*

> him, "Every man serves the good wine first, and when the people have drunk freely, then he serves the poorer wine; but you have kept the good wine until now." John 2:7-10

My first "sermon" taught me the invaluable life lesson that my skill or talent (or lack thereof) wasn't the issue with God. What He desired was an open vessel, yes clay, maybe even a little cracked, but empty, so to be filled by His Word and His Spirit. A pot filled with our own vision, ideas, even teachings won't have room for His plan for us. He'd much rather we be weak and broken than full of ourselves.

The ingredient Jesus would have for us as His vessels would be to be filled to the brim with His Word (primarily the Bible, but also the prophetic word) and the Holy Spirit.

Of course, continuing with the illustration or living parable, full pots must be poured, emptied before being filled, again and again. What a waste to pour into a full vessel.

Being involved in the miraculous is the process of pouring out and being refilled. Like manna, it would be nice to store it somewhere, but that is not how it works.

We have to have a way of "filling back up" after we have been used. This is where many ministers make a drastic mistake. They continue trying to minister in their own strength after the anointing is gone. We are created as triune beings—body, soul, and spirit. We must take time to make sure that all our "pots" are filled up—spiritually, physically, and emotionally. While the Spirit of God overcomes much of our human weakness, it is not healthy to neglect the physical or emotional side of our being. Too often, physical weariness and emotional emptiness has led to depression, burnout, and gross sin in the lives of those who are genuinely being used in the ministry.

My Jakarta days

Julie and I had the privilege of living in the great city of Jakarta, Indonesia for over three years. During those years we had the incredible joy of serving our Gereja Pantekosta di Indonesia Foursquare churches, that numbered over 18,000 at that time and have continued to increase daily to this day. I absolutely loved those years as I love beyond measure my Indonesian brothers and sisters. Their heart and passion to preach the gospel has been a constant source of inspiration to me.

My Indonesian friends so love the Lord that it seems they are having services of one kind or another almost every day of the week. With our great relationship and mutual love for one another it seemed I had the opportunity to minister together with them somewhere on an almost daily basis. I remember one month where I actually ministered the delivery of around fifty 60 to 90 minute messages.

Well, after that kind of schedule, I remember coming away feeling like I was a "preaching machine" that is just turned on and off to blast out another message. It is still so vivid in my memory. One particular overcast afternoon, I was back home in our apartment in the Jakarta CBD. We lived up on the 33rd floor overlooking all the beautiful sky rise buildings of the city.

For some reason I was feeling really, really down, although everything in the natural was going great as far as the ministry goes. Maybe it was just because Julie was away ministering, and I had been giving so much of myself, that it caused a wave of depression to come over me. I cried out, "Lord, is this it? Where is the touch of your Spirit? I see you touching those I speak to and pray for, but I feel absolutely empty."

Immediately I heard the gentle voice of the Holy Spirit telling me, "It is because you haven't spent time with me." I had to acknowledge this was the absolute sober truth. It seemed that my busyness doing the work of God was giving me the excuse to avoid my personal relationship with Him. With that wake up call I immediately went to my knees and then to a time of worship and praying in the Spirit. With that intensity it seemed that 15 minutes had hardly passed and I was instantly filled with new joy, peace, and boldness to continue on in the work of the ministry.

Staying full takes some effort on our part. We often need to push through the physical weariness and emotional drain brought on by the spiritual battle around us. The spiritual disciplines of Bible study, prayer, fasting, worship, faithfulness, and fellowship renew and strengthen our spiritual beings. Paul encourages us to "walk in the Spirit, and you won't fulfill the lusts of the flesh." (Galatians 5:16)

A friend of mine has an excellent personal example of this principle. I'll let him share his story in his own words:

> *I was pastoring a church in a rural community and leading a team of three couples that ministered in a state correctional facility. We did two services every Monday night. To make a long story short, a man in prison (who was supposed to be a brother in Christ) decided to steal my wife. Behind my back he set about seducing her and, when he was released from prison, she ran off with him to another state, leaving me without a wife and our three teen-aged children without a mother. Not sure what the future held, I tried to maintain an example of love, patience, and faithfulness to my children, to our church, and to my ministry. I wanted them to know that you didn't have to quit because bad things happened to you.*
>
> *A couple of weeks after she left I went back to minister at the prison as usual. I sat in the front row of the chapel during the worship service. Honestly I felt like road kill. I didn't want to be there. It was everything I could do not to turn the service over to the worship leader and walk out to go sit in the car until they had finished— but I didn't.*

I had nothing to say to these men—many who knew what had happened. I sat there battling fatigue and emotional pain and emptiness as I was praying, asking God to do something in spite of me. In a few minutes I would have to stand up and share something profound (as preachers often feel pressured to do). The worship service ended and I stood to "minister." I don't remember what I preached that night, but I remember opening my mouth and then I spoke the first word the Spirit of God poured out on me, in me, and through me. We had a tremendous service with many men being touched by the Spirit of God. In my experience, the discipline of faithfulness kept me filled, even when I couldn't feel it in the midst of the spiritual battle swirling around me. The anointing that flowed through me that night not only washed away much of the hurt and confusion, but left me renewed in spirit and mind. I have often wondered what would have happened in my life if I had walked out of that service.

The 4th Ingredient: Keep Full of the Word and Spirit

Jesus said to them, "Fill the waterpots with water." So they filled them up to the brim. John 2:7

In the Bible, the Word and the Spirit of God are often alluded to by references to water. For instance, Paul tells us that we are "sanctified and washed by the water of the Word." In John chapter 7, Jesus speaks of believing in Him, drinking the water He gives, and having "rivers of living water flow from our innermost being." John goes on to interpret the statement, "But this He spoke of the Spirit."

The Word and the Spirit go together in the miraculous realm. Simply think back to the story of creation. The Spirit brooded over the waters and the spoken Word created everything. So we find that the "water" He fills us with is the Word and the Holy Spirit. I like that! The fact that they filled them to the brim—to the point where if there was any more they would be overflowing—is significant. I think that's how we need to be when it comes to the Word of God and the Holy Spirit in our life. I've noticed that the people who are filled with the Word, and are filled constantly to the point of overflowing with the Holy Spirit, are the same kind of people that seem to have a lot more breakthroughs and miracles.

A second principle to be learned here is that religious legalism will never produce a miracle. As mentioned, these pots were "religious" pots (thankfully they were not cracked, or we would have to discuss religious crack-pots). They were there for legalistic ritual washing as prescribed by the Law of Moses. It is the Spirit of God that imparts the gifts and does the work, not our self-righteousness or self-effort, born of legalistic religious observances.

Paul addressed the Galatian Christians who were being seduced back into legalism by the Jews. In Galatians chapter 3, he challenged these saints to avoid the snare of legalism. First he asked them if they received the Spirit of God by faith or by legalistic observances. Then he pressed the issue and asked if those working miracles among them did it by the religious efforts of the law or by faith.

Likewise, Peter and John testified to the uselessness of religious works in Acts chapter 3 when the lame man was healed. Peter dismissed their own power or righteousness as means of producing the miracle, and instead pointed to God Himself as the source of healing.

> *Then Peter said, "Silver and gold have I none; but such as I have give I thee: In the name of Jesus Christ of Nazareth rise up and walk." Acts 3:6 KJV*

My friend who shared the earlier story also shared about another event at the same prison.

> *We were holding a service in the medium security side of the prison. All evening long I kept looking at a man on the front row who had just arrived in the prison that morning. He looked to be one of the most miserable persons I had ever seen. We went through worship and then I shared the Word of God with the group gathered, but I couldn't really get past this man on the front row. As I ended the message and gave an altar call I*

asked this young man if he would let me pray for him. He agreed and stood up. I asked our team and some of the Christian prisoners in the service to gather around him as we prayed. There were probably twenty or thirty gathered around at the front of the chapel. I laid hands on him and felt the Spirit direct me to cast a demon out of him. He was standing with his head hanging down slightly bent forward, totally dejected. I began praying the typical prayer of deliverance and suddenly he threw his head back so hard his glasses flew up and hit the ceiling. When he did, he let out a prolonged blood-curdling scream and stood there with his back arched backwards screaming at the ceiling. This was disconcerting enough in and of itself. But to make matters worse, I was standing in a chapel in the middle of a medium security prison with guards wandering around just outside the doors.

I commanded the demon to leave him—he kept screaming. I did it again and then again—he kept screaming. I knew we would have guards rushing in the place in a few seconds and I would probably have a lot of explaining to do to the warden. (It wouldn't be the first time I got called to the warden's office.)

The thought went through my head, "This is not working, you are failing and you'll look like a fool and will probably get in trouble to boot." I shoved that thought out of my head and said, "I said in JESUS' name shut up and come out of him." The man dropped to the floor instantly, unconscious and silent.

A few seconds later several guards came in the back door and demanded to know what was happening. Since the scene had gone quiet and we had 30 people at the altar, and they couldn't see the man on the floor, I said, "Sorry officers, we were just praying, everything is okay." They left and the man got up, transformed by the power of God. This was a real object lesson for me.

I was depending on my "ability" to pray for this man's deliverance. I had done it before and was following the same pattern. My "method" and rote prayer was failing. I could have caved into the thoughts going through my mind, but the Spirit of God encouraged me to trust Jesus fully. It truly was not my own righteousness or power that set the man free—and this is exactly what God wanted me to learn from the experience.

The principle to remember is that staying in the Word of God and maintaining a Spiritual life will keep us from reverting to religious words and activities, and provide an atmosphere that is conducive for God to work miracles in and through your life. Remember that it is always the power given to us by the Holy Spirit.

> *"Not by might nor by power, but by My Spirit," says the Lord of hosts. Zechariah 4:6*

Chapter 6

THE POSITION OF EXPECTING

Miracle Ingredient 5 of 7: Consider Your Miracle Is On Its Way

"Your daughter will die. There is no hope."

The doctor's words hung in the air; he didn't attempt to lessen their weight.

In that moment, the most crushing moment Julie and I had ever experienced, I could feel my faith pour out from my soul and spirit. We were both numb, anesthetized by the power of the crushing report.

My wife and I were in our early twenties, young pastors in Tucson, Arizona—full of dreams of serving God and to soon see our expected baby girl.

I worked extra hard and did little side jobs wherever I could so that

Our daughter was on life support, so many wires and monitors on her that I had trouble reaching my hands through the enclosed plexiglass bed.

I could save enough money to pay for all of Julie's prenatal care and for the delivery, doctor, and hospital fees. I remember being so proud of myself that I was able to take care of everything, expense-wise, before our baby was even born.

After talking with one of our friends who was an insurance agent, he congratulated me on taking care of everything upfront, but encouraged me to take out a separate insurance policy just in case anything went wrong with either Julie or the baby during delivery. I went ahead and paid for his insurance policy just in case something happened that was not covered. However, after a few months, I started feeling really unsettled inside of myself. I felt that if I were a man of faith, I certainly wouldn't be planning for disaster with my wife and soon-to-be-born baby. Zealous, but immature and anxious, I cancelled our policy.

Our daughter, named Jocelyn, decided to come prematurely. Immediately after Julie gave birth, the nurses took our daughter away from us without explaining what was wrong. They then took our newborn off by emergency transport to another hospital for specialized care. It was apparently the best hospital in the city to deal with premature infants. They have specialists for every problem, including the heart and lungs in premature children. We rushed ourselves immediately to that hospital, where in absolute agony we waited to hear what was wrong with our newborn baby.

Hearing the horrible news, a group in our church held a special prayer meeting for Jocelyn. They prayed, taking a piece of cloth, anointing it with oil, and placing their hands on it. That same night they brought the cloth to Julie and me, pleading with us to take it to our daughter and place it upon her dying body. I knew the New Testament story of the prayer cloth, but it seemed strange, even unnecessary. At first I was reluctant, wondering why we were in the situation in the first place and why God allowed this to happen to people who believe in Him so faithfully. I kicked and screamed in my heart, then made my decision that we would go and pray and try again, believing for a breakthrough.

Our daughter was on life support, so many wires and monitors on her that I had trouble reaching my hands through the enclosed plexiglass bed. As soon as I placed the cloth on her body and prayed, something happened immediately. The nurses came in and very rudely and abruptly chased us away. They weren't sure what we had done, but seemed to be angry with us and made us leave. After waiting for some time, very scared and not knowing what happened with our daughter, the nurses finally came out. They apologized to us and told us they were sorry to have chased us away. They explained that they thought we had done something to the monitors, because for some reason, all her vital signs suddenly changed to completely normal. They told us that they then called in a number of doctors to verify this and to see what had happened.

All the doctors confirmed that our daughter's vital signs were normal for a newborn baby. With that, the nurses informed us that there was no reason for them to keep our daughter in the hospital, other than the fact that the hospital policy required that they keep her overnight just to see if anything changed by morning.

Julie and I were absolutely overjoyed and beside ourselves, knowing that the Lord had done something mighty in our midst. We came early in the morning to receive our new baby girl. We were so overjoyed with this miracle and with the opportunity to tell everyone what God had done. Even in the midst of a miracle, the everyday issues of life can confront us. I knew that even though I had paid all the bills for the prenatal care, hospital, and delivery, I still had massive bills to pay for the special treatment, transportation, and other expenses. Still, I was so overjoyed with the miracle of our daughter's healing that I really didn't care what the bills were.

Once the baby was handed to Julie, I was asked to go see the hospital administrator before checking out. The administrator, probably feeling proud and attributing this great miracle to the staff of nurses and doctors at the hospital, brought me in and presented me with my bill. I explained to her that though there was no way for me to pay at the moment, that I was a man of faith and of my word and would absolutely pay my bill, even if it took me my whole life.

While I was still speaking to her, a knock came on the door of the office. A man came in and spoke quietly to the hospital administrator, handing what looked like a file of some sort to her for her review, and then turned and went out the door. After looking things over, the hospital administrator gave us news we could hardly believe—our bills were paid in full. Apparently, many years before, an older gentleman had left money to the hospital for cases just like ours. Our daughter's sickness, transportation, and every other detail just happened to fit the requirements and instructions on how to use the money.

When we left the hospital, that was the happiest day we had ever experienced. We had a beautiful, healthy baby girl, a great testimony of a miracle, and all our bills were paid. I still go back and remember those faithful saints who prayed for our daughter and absolutely believed that if we just placed that prayer cloth upon her she would be completely healed. Those faithful saints considered that the miracle was already done and all we had to do was be obedient.

The 5th Ingredient: Consider Your Miracle Is On Its Way

And He said to them, "Draw some out now and take it to the headwaiter." So they took it to him.
John 2:8

We don't know what, if anything, was going through the minds of the servants that Jesus instructed. One wonders at first if they might have been reluctant to take what they knew was water to the master of the feast who was expecting more wine.

Just like the servants who dutifully obeyed, sometimes we are called to believe, yes, even expect, before the miracle has arrived. Some spell faith r-i-s-k. The servants could have been ridiculed and admonished at best, beaten at worst, should the miracle have never happened.

Yet, like Peter contemplating the storm and the water below him, they stepped out. Why?

Because Jesus told them to and Mary gave them permission.

And it's interesting to note that Mary's faith in Jesus' ability also "gave faith" to the servants to fulfill their task—just like our faithful prayer warriors with their prayer cloth. We all believed, but their push at a critical time was essential to Julie and me, restoring our faith and then helping us to step out in it—even though all the circumstances cried out to say "Stop!"

Mary knew Jesus. She knew His character; therefore, she could take comfort in the fact that the miracle was already done. Even after He protested, "What does your concern have to do with me?

> *He* is willing, able, and takes great joy in showing His love and care for us even at the most difficult times of our lives.

My hour has not yet come." She simply said to the servants, "Whatever He says to you, do it." She trusted Jesus, she stepped out even when she could have easily recoiled and dropped the matter.

When people, like Mary, have that kind of determination, it seems that God honors it. He honored it throughout scripture.

I imagine that Jesus, upon hearing His mother's words and before He instructed the servants, had even the slightest smile on His face. Oh that the Lord should smile upon us when we believe for Him to come through.

Still Hope in God

I remember a woman in California not far from where we lived. This woman had come down with cancer and after going to the doctor and being opened up, the doctor immediately closed her up and told her she only had a few months to live. She accepted the fact that she would die, but continued to pray and ask the Lord to touch her and give her more time. One day, after praying, she felt the Lord tell her that He was going to heal her, and that assuredly she would not die. She immediately went to her husband and told him the great news. Her husband was so excited and believed in faith for this breakthrough for his wife. However, as the days went on she began to lose more and more weight and every sign pointed to the fact that the cancer was draining the life out of her body.

Her husband, broken-hearted, began to give up. But this dear woman refused to quit. She was so certain that she had heard from the Lord that she would not stop claiming that the Lord would heal her. As the days went on she became so weak and frail that her family actually started preparing for her funeral. However, she kept on believing in the words the Lord spoke to her. The date by which her doctor had expected her to die came and went. She noticed that she had begun to regain some of her strength. She started to get an appetite again and she put on weight. Finally, she went back to her doctor and asked for another checkup to ascertain her present condition. The doctor was absolutely amazed to find during the checkup that there was no cancer in her body anymore. What an amazing thing it is to watch how, even when there is no hope in the natural realm, there is still hope in God.

Abraham demonstrated this principle in his life in a wonderful way:

> *A father of many nations have I made you in the sight of Him whom he believed, even God, who gives life to the dead and calls into being that which does not exist. In hope against hope he believed, in order that he might become a father of many nations, according to that which had been spoken, "So shall your descendants be." And without becoming weak in faith he contemplated his own body, now as good as dead since he was*

> *about a hundred years old, and the deadness of Sarah's womb; yet, with respect to the promise of God, he did not waver in unbelief, but grew strong in faith, giving glory to God, and being fully assured that what He had promised, He was able also to perform. Romans 4:17-21*

You have to know that age, life circumstance, or any doctor's diagnosis cannot stop the hand of the God of the miraculous whom we serve. He is willing, able, and takes great joy in showing His love and care for us even at the most difficult times of our lives.

> *For the eyes of the Lord move to and fro throughout the earth that He may strongly support those whose heart is completely His.*
> *1 Chronicles 16:9*

Chapter 7

THE POSITION OF BELIEVING

Miracle Ingredient 6 of 7: Add a Measure of Faith

Some miracles make you cringe.

While we were serving as pastors to a church in Southern California, there was a woman in our congregation who seemed to be the perfect parishioner. She was always faithful to attend both the Sunday morning and the Wednesday night services. She faithfully gave her tithes and offerings and never complained about anything. However, I did notice that she never seemed comfortable during services, even in our extra plush, green padded pews. She frequently shifted her weight and moved from side to side during sermons.

One Wednesday night she stayed seated until everyone else had gone home. The only other person in the church was my assistant pastor. We were just about to shut everything down after the service when she came

> *T*he power that manifested had an effect on me. I found that I could hardly walk…

to the front and told me her story. She said, "Pastor, have you noticed that I'm in a great deal of pain?" I acknowledged that I had noticed this, and that she seemed uncomfortable sitting, especially during my lengthier sermons.

She told me how her spine had undergone such degeneration that she lived in constant and severe pain. She explained that she was both in physical therapy and on strong pain medication, but that nothing helped. She had asked her doctor for an even stronger medication, but he refused, telling her there was nothing more that he could do.

At that moment, her faith rose up within her. She told her doctor, "If there's nothing you can do, then I'm going to my pastor this Wednesday night at church, and when he prays for me, I will be healed." The doctor had immediately replied that he didn't believe in miracles. After relating this story, she looked at me, closed her eyes, leaned her head toward me and said, "Go ahead, Pastor, just pray for me." I hesitated for a moment, and feeling this hesitation, she said again, "Pray for me."

I have never witnessed such amazing faith and assurance that someone would get their miracle. After taking some anointing oil, I reached out and barely touched her forehead. To my absolute amazement, I saw something that I had never seen before.

When I touched her, something picked her up off the ground and threw her back several feet, slamming her to the floor on the center aisle of the church. She hit the floor so hard that I could feel the vibration all the way back to where I was standing. I thought to myself that if her back weren't bad before, it would be now.

I turned to my assistant pastor and told him, "I didn't do that!" I thought for sure that as hard as she hit the floor she certainly must be dead. Again I looked at my assistant pastor, "You saw that. I didn't do that." I decided to wait 30 seconds and then call an ambulance. After the 30 seconds were up, we went to examine what looked like a lifeless body. I asked her if she was okay. Her eyes were closed, but the slight crack of a smile came upon her face. I asked if I could help her up. She quickly told me, "No," and that she wanted to get up by herself, which she proceeded to do. She got up slowly, leaned forward, and then backward, and then began to jump up and down, declaring that she was healed.

The power that manifested had an effect on me. I found that I could hardly walk, and I was woozy and disoriented. This has since happened several times after a great healing. It was almost as if some of the power of God was still left in my body as it had passed through me to the woman. I have heard that this phenomenon has occurred with others who have been used as vessels of healing, and sometimes the effect has lasted for days. We can certainly take no credit when a miracle occurs, but we can enjoy the results of being a conduit of the power of the Holy Spirit.

This woman was so excited that she went to her doctor to tell him about her incredible miracle. He immediately told her again, "I don't believe in miracles. You're just having a good day. I can promise you that the pain will return." Over a period of months, she continued to ask her doctor if he would release her and allow her to return to work. He continued to refuse until finally she demanded an x-ray of her back. He finally agreed. He pulled out the old x-ray and compared the two. He was so amazed that he said, "I told you I don't believe in miracles. I still don't believe in miracles, but you got one." He signed the release form which enabled her to go back to work and live a normal life. To this day, I have never seen such absolute faith like that in anyone. She *knew* that if she came to Jesus, He would heal her.

The 6th Ingredient: Add a Measure of Faith

> *When the headwaiter tasted the water which had become wine, and did not know where it came from (but the servants who had drawn the water knew), the headwaiter called the bridegroom. John 2:9*

Imagine, the master of the feast bringing the cup of freshly fetched wine to his lips. For that split second, what do you think raced through the minds of the servants standing nearby? "If it's still water, he'll spit it out, be embarrassed, and we're in big trouble!" They might have witnessed the color change but who knows if someone just added some food coloring, or a first century version of Kool-

Aid. Maybe I'm not giving them enough credit. But I'm certain those servants carefully studied the master's face as he swallowed the liquid.

He called for the bridegroom. "Now we're really dead," they might have thought. Good chance the master kept a straight face until he could express his joy to the bridegroom. The master, unaware of Jesus' miracle, gave the joyful proclamation, "You have kept the good wine until now!"

The servants probably looked at each other, smiling even while they exhaled. Time to party.

Faith is the critical ingredient to any miracle, yet as this scripture shows, it isn't always front and center. Yes, Mary had faith. Even those poor servants had to have a measure of faith. But it is always God who does the miracle.

When I pray for the sick, the "pressure" is not on me—it's on God. It's for Him to decide to move or not. If I took on that pressure, that responsibility for the thousands I've individually prayed for, I'd be begging for early retirement.

And yet, I'm always wanting to be in the position for seeing Him move, and that position is one of belief, belief that Jesus is the same yesterday, today, and forever. (Hebrews 13:8)

Real Faith

While this book is meant to help you increase your faith, it is important to consider what faith really is. There is a real faith and there is a phony faith. In both 1 and 2 Timothy, Paul uses the phrase "unfeigned faith," or, as some modern translations put it, "sincere faith." This would seem to indicate that there is a fake or insincere faith—a "faith" borne of false motives and false methods.

I grew up in the years when the subject of faith was the most common message you heard coming from the platform. It seemed that every time you turned on the television someone was preaching on increasing your faith. While it is true that "without faith it is impossible to please God," (Hebrews 11:6) it seemed to me the entire subject was wrongly taught and abused. If you didn't have enough faith, there was always someone willing to sell you some of theirs. You could buy it in bottles of water, bottles of anointing oil, prayer cloths, or a signed copy of their latest book. We said things like "just name it and claim it," or "confess it and possess it." In many cases it became about material possessions for the hearers and a means to get an offering for the preachers.

> There is even a higher purpose of faith. There is faith that is not self-absorbed with a materialistic orientation. It is a faith that is for the benefit of others…

One of the funniest stories I can recall is about a friend of mine from church who had an older Mercedes Benz. It was one of the old diesels that you had to shut the air-conditioning off upon acceleration if you wanted the car to move. This old friend had been dreaming about one of the new models he had seen in the latest car magazine. One day while at his house, I saw a picture of the new model, the big 560 SEL. All I knew about it was that it was big, blue, beautiful, and full of every kind of luxury inside.

What interested me more was the driver in the photo. It was my friend inside this beautiful car. I then looked a bit closer and realized how he got in the driver's seat. My friend had cut out a small photo of himself and carefully glued it on so it looked like he was driving the car. I said, "What is this all about?" He said, "That's my car. Every time I come to the fridge I see that photo and I claim it in Jesus' Name!"

At that point I said to myself, "Well, really, I doubt that will ever happen." Not long after this, I got a knock at my door. When I opened it, it was my friend standing there with a great big smile on his face. I said, "What's going on?" Immediately he said, "I got it, I got the car!" I remember thinking to myself, "No way!" But as I walked outside, there it was, the car from the magazine, or at least one that looked just like it, sitting in my driveway. I couldn't believe it. I know that God is a God of extreme blessing and certainly provided richly for so many throughout the scriptures. Yet I have never really gotten into that kind of faith, as so many did in my generation, because the faith exhibited by Jesus and His disciples was so focused upon "the least of these."

Well, I don't know how it worked out, but I did notice my same friend was driving a Ford about six months later. I didn't dare ask what happened to the beautiful Mercedes, but rather felt that was between him and God. I will say, though, that I am absolutely overjoyed when the people of God are overwhelmingly blessed. Many of my friends have been blessed beyond measure and it gives me great joy when I see it. I have personally witnessed these precious men and women of God being showered with blessings because they "seek first His Kingdom and His righteousness, and (have found) all these things will be added" (Matthew 6:33) as well.

There is even a higher purpose of faith. There is faith that is not self-absorbed with a materialistic orientation. It is a faith that is for the benefit of others, a faith that changes lives and impacts entire tribes, people groups, and nations, a faith to see the devil uprooted in individual lives, families, and even geographical areas.

The ministry of missions is full of stories of those who went and served—and sometimes died—in faith without seeing much of an impact. Yet the seeds of their faith paved the way for others to come reap a rich harvest for the Kingdom of God. They could be easily listed with the names in Hebrews chapter 11, of whom it was said, "All these died in faith, not having received the promise."

> *F*aith is the currency in the economy of the Kingdom of God.

The Story of Jim Elliot, as related in the book *Through Gates of Splendor,* is one such example. In Ecuador, Jim and four other missionaries were killed by Huaorani tribesmen during the time the missionaries were trying to evangelize the tribe. Later, Elliot's wife and other missionaries went back and continued evangelistic efforts and reached the tribe for Jesus. Even the man who killed Jim Elliot came to know Jesus.

Richard and June Bartz, missionaries to South East Asia, told a more recent story. The Bartzes spent six years in one such country and had one convert to show for it. Richard tells the story in his January 2015 mission newsletter:

> *Twenty-three years ago we could not openly proclaim the gospel in the country we were serving. We used to walk around different neighborhoods at night praying for the day when the truth could be openly preached and people could hear and respond to the love of God. It seemed impossible at the time but we prayed anyway.*
>
> *The place where we lived was very closed to Christianity. Churches were burned and never could be rebuilt. It was a hard place! However, on December 1, 2014 there was a public evangelistic meeting held there and an estimated 4,000 people attended. Most of the people who came were of another religious belief. A former fanatic who had even killed and burned his Christian victims before Jesus changed his life*

> *was preaching the gospel. There was a great response, many received Christ, some were healed, and many fell to the ground as the presence of God fell on them. There were only two military guards present, yet there was no violence or protests at all! We thank God for answered prayer – our prayer and those of so many others who hoped for this day! A month later the government started relocating some refugees to this area. These refugees tended to be very radical and began to severely persecute the Christians. The spiritual warfare in this area is great, but the prayers of the saints make a strategic difference.*

One error of the whole faith movement and message was to condemn, or to produce condemnation, in those who didn't "possess what they confessed." There is a real balance to faith. Sometimes those who remain steadfast in their belief, even when they don't see the thing they believed for, express the greatest faith. They are convinced and convicted of the truth, though they may never see it. Sometimes God gives you the faith for something that others will see in the future.

In the Book of Hebrews, chapter 11, we have an interesting commentary on faith. Here, the names of those that didn't get what they believed for are listed. Yet the Bible said, "They died in faith," and "The world was not worthy of them," and that all those listed had "gained approval through their faith."

> *All these died in faith, without receiving the promises, but having seen them and having welcomed them from a distance, and having confessed that they were strangers and exiles on the earth. Hebrews 11:13*

> *They were stoned, they were sawn in two, they were tempted, they were put to death with the sword; they went about in sheepskins, in goatskins, being destitute, afflicted, ill-treated (men of whom the world was not worthy), wandering in deserts and mountains and caves and holes in the ground. And all these, <u>having gained approval through their faith</u>… Hebrews 11:38-39*

Faith is the currency in the economy of the Kingdom of God. There is something about this faith thing that moves God.

> *What then shall we say that Abraham, our forefather, discovered in this matter? If, in fact, Abraham was justified by works, he had something to boast about—but not before God. What does the Scripture say? "Abraham believed God, and it was credited to him as righteousness." Romans 4:1-3 NIV*

Abraham believed God and it was credited to him for righteousness and he became the "Father of Faith" to all who believe. We need to get this. Abraham's righteousness was not about his moral or religious observances. God accepted Abraham's faith in the place of morality or religious observances.

Jesus said, "Be it done according to your faith." Jesus most certainly had faith, but it appears that he also knew those who had, and did not have, faith.

> *Now faith is the substance of things hoped for, the evidence of things not seen. Hebrews 11:1 KJV*

The writer of Hebrews tries to convey the idea of what faith really is in terms that we can understand. He says that faith is the "substance of things hoped for." In the best possible case, faith is intangible. Yet the writer declares faith to be as solid as the thing which we are believing to be made manifest. The Greek word he uses is *hupostasis* (hoop-os'-tas-is); and it means a setting under the concrete, the foundation that things are built on (support confidence, substance). Genuine faith is a sure foundation that God builds on.

He also tells us that faith is "the evidence of things not seen." Evidence is material fact used to convince someone of the reality or truthfulness of a thing. It is proof positive that something is so. How can something you cannot see be evidence? Yet the writer is very emphatic that we understand that faith is so solid that it replaces the material reality and the proof, which we cannot yet see. Faith is the "placeholder," so to speak, until the manifested reality comes into being.

The truth is we often get what we can believe for. The Bible indicates that faith is quantitative. Paul and Jesus used the word "measure" when speaking of faith. Paul tells us in Romans 12 that every one of us has been given a "measure of faith," and that we are to use it to minister accordingly. Jesus chided his disciples for having "a little faith" but not enough to calm the storm themselves. In other places in the Bible, Jesus spoke of "great faith." Upon seeing a dramatic exorcism, the disciples asked Jesus to "increase our faith."

All of these words and phrases indicate that God initially imparts faith to a person, but that faith can be "increased." Because of this, there are two very important principles that we must develop in our faith-walk.

The first is: Use the faith you have been given. It is a sure bet that your faith will not increase if you don't use it.

The second is: Stretch your faith to cause it to grow. We all have been dealt a measure of faith, according to Paul. We tend to be comfortable in that realm. However, for our faith to grow and become stronger it requires that we get out of our faith comfort-zone and take some risks. In fact, faith is really all about risks. According to Paul, it believes in something you cannot yet see and for which you have no evidence. Faith means you do not have the wherewithal to do something in your own power and ability and, that if God doesn't come through, nothing is going to happen. The old cliché, "a leap of faith," is quite appropriate in this situation. Every leap requires a platform to jump from. In this case it is our existing faith. The Bible admonishes us to grow from "faith to faith."

Increasing your faith is critical if you want to see miracles. Early in Jesus' ministry He went to his hometown to minister. The old saying, "familiarity breeds contempt," seems to be a reality here. The people heard Jesus, but wrote him off as someone they all knew. Even though they acknowledged his wisdom and "miraculous powers" they were offended at him and refused to believe. Matthew wrote the sad commentary on the situation: "And he did not do many miracles there because of their lack of faith." (Matthew 13:58)

I'll add a side note here: Offense will destroy your ability to believe. Many people are angry with God for one reason or another. Perhaps it was some hard-to-understand circumstance, like the untimely death of a loved one, or a debilitating disease that came out of nowhere. Perhaps it was an unanswered prayer or years of abuse at the hands of another.

No matter what the circumstance, people tend to blame God, either directly or indirectly, for the problem and get offended at Him. Some directly accuse God by saying, "Why did God do this to me?" Others blame God indirectly by saying, "Why did God allow this to happen to me?" We often hear someone say, "Where was God when I was suffering?" Or, "Why doesn't God do something about all the wickedness and child abuse and poverty and famine?"

The bottom line for those offended at God is that they cannot and will not believe because they have already judged Him to be uncaring or impotent. If you find yourself needing a miracle, but have become offended at God, I urge you with everything in me to reconcile with the God who loves you so much that He was willing to die for you, rather than to allow you to spend eternity apart from Him. God is not the author of your confusion. Satan is. Make things right with God and let go of whatever supposed grievance you have and open the door to faith once again.

Chapter 8

THE POSITION OF SERVING
Miracle Ingredient 7 of 7: Mix in Some Compassion

Driving through Papua New Guinea is never a leisurely sightseeing tour. The roads are rough with holes that can swallow you whole and are littered with the carcasses of cars that failed to make it out alive, picked clean by the mechanical vultures that lie in wait.

Then there are the robbers, or "rascals" as they are called, ready to pounce, day or night. They can emerge suddenly from the tall grasslands like locust upon the crops.

Yet the people are beautiful, wonderful testimonies of God's grace and I never tire of seeing their faces and embracing their genuine love. As I entered the church, leaving the cool breeze, I was moved by their presence.

I read from Psalm 23 and then told a personal story, no doubt

> *The servant operates in humility and obedience, not drawing attention to himself.*

inspired by the cars left on the side of the road I had just traveled.

"He restores my soul," I reminded the people, repeating the scripture. I went on to share of my hobby of restoring old, beaten up cars to the way they originally looked. "I love to see an old, worthless car come alive, made beautiful once again."

I went on to say, "I saw this car once and I had to have it. Friends, even my wife, asked why—it was such a worthless piece of junk. But I saw what it could become.

"So I bought it and put my hands on every single part of it and made it the way it was originally designed to be. Once I finished, everyone was amazed that such a neglected and cast aside car could look and run so beautifully again. Over and over I got the comments, 'I wish I could have a car like that.'"

I could sense the Lord was moving through my words. The transition from cars to these people was seamless.

"The Lord wants to restore your soul. He wants to put His hands on every part of your mind, emotions, and will. Where you have been robbed, hurt, abused, He will restore hope and joy and love."

As I continued, the sound began. It was the wailing of deep pain being released to God. Every one of the women in that church began to howl, pulling their dresses over their heads as if to make their moment with God private.

Strangely, the men just watched in amazement wondering what was happening to their women. It was as if the Lord had gathered these ladies into one big, corporate hug whispering to them, "I see your worth. I see your value. I am restoring you."

Many of the women throughout Papua New Guinea have experienced some form of abuse. Jesus swept in and delivered them that day. The pastor and national leader, Timothy Tipitap, was so moved, telling me later that he'd never seen anything like that before.

I didn't need to individually pray for any of them, the Spirit of God had already moved. It was a miracle of the restored soul.

The 7th Ingredient: Mix in Some Compassion

The often overlooked ingredient from the wedding at Cana is compassion. The culture that Jesus lived within was what missionaries call "shame based." In other words, the culture, Semitic, was founded on the premise that bringing shame to your family was the worst offense. If you sinned, that was one thing, but if your sin brought shame to your family, that was an entirely worse matter.

Mary knew that for the bridal party to run out of wine before the evening was over was a big social faux pas. It would bring shame to this family. Today, we might laugh it off and tell folks, "We're sorry." But for a first century Jewish family, that was a very unpleasant option.

In fact, the motivation of Jesus' first miracle was compassion—first pointed out by Mary and finally carried out by Jesus, and of course with an assist from the servants.

The servants were the only ones who saw the miracle and took part in it, even though everyone benefited from it. Having a servant's heart is paramount to seeing miracles. The servant operates in humility and obedience, not drawing attention to himself. In fact, this attitude was at the very heart of Jesus' life and ministry.

> *Have this attitude in yourselves which was also in Christ Jesus, who, although He existed in the form of God, did not regard equality with God a thing to be grasped, but emptied Himself, taking the form of a bond-servant, and being made in the likeness of men. Being found in appearance as a man, He humbled Himself by becoming obedient to the point of death, even death on a cross. For this reason also, God highly exalted Him, and bestowed on Him the name which is above every name.*
> Philippians 2:5-9

You see, everywhere Jesus went he was ministering to people. Yes, His message was to repent and believe the gospel, but He was actively ministering, healing, and bringing freedom from demonic oppression and bondage to those who would believe in Him.

Several times we are told Jesus had "compassion" on the people and ministered to them out of that compassion. We are told He was "moved with compassion" and even wept over the brokenness of the people.

The greatest miracles often happen because someone has reached out in compassion and cared enough for someone else to sacrifice their own time, energy, and comfort to make a difference in someone else's life. This compassionate servanthood was the foundation of Jesus' ministry. Jesus was modeling the principle that "faith works through love."

> *There is a dynamic flow of kingdom power and resource that takes place when God's people serve others with faith and compassion.*

Again, Jesus started His ministry with a proclamation from Isaiah:

> *The Spirit of the Lord is upon Me, because He anointed Me to preach the gospel to the poor. He has sent Me to proclaim release to the captives, and recovery of sight to the blind, to set free those who are oppressed, to proclaim the favorable year of the Lord. Isaiah 61:1-2a*

I believe we are still in that day, "The favorable year of the Lord." I believe it is still in His heart to serve people and that it is this heart that opens the windows of Heaven and makes Heaven's resources available to those who are compassionately serving God, by serving God's people.

Matthew relates the story of Jesus teaching and healing the multitude that came to him. The disciples reminded Jesus that they were in a remote place and that the people would need to go away and buy food. They urged Jesus to send them away. Now the disciples were genuinely concerned about the people. They knew they would be hungry and that they would have to journey, and that if they didn't leave soon they would not be able to buy food for their families that night.

Jesus was also concerned for the people, but took a different strategy. He told the disciples not to send them away but to give them something to eat. It is one thing to see a need and another to do something about it. The disciples based their response on their lack, while Jesus based his response on faith. They had all the resources they needed; they just needed to mix it with compassionate faith and obedience to minister to the needs of the people.

When did the power come? When did the miracle happen? It wasn't when Jesus prayed; it was when the disciples started handing out the few fish and loaves. When Jesus handed it back to them, there were still only a few fish and a couple loaves of bread. As they obeyed in faith, the miracle happened. It is doubtful that the multitude even knew what was happening, but the disciples (servants) did.

There is a dynamic flow of kingdom power and resource that takes place when God's people serve others with faith and compassion. Remember, the Word says, "Faith works by love."

I think of my good friends, Drs. Ted and Sue Olbrich, in Cambodia who planted thousands of churches and built orphan homes, and have experienced over a half million people coming to the Lord. It all started because of their faith and compassion to serve a few widows and orphans. Their ministry opened the doors for the power of Heaven to flow into that nation.

I think about the amazing story of Abraham in Genesis. Abraham called his servant and charged him to return to his homeland and to his family to find a wife for his son, Isaac. The servant prayed that God would give him a sign of God's good favor by pointing out the girl God had chosen to be Isaac's wife. He dictated the conditions to God, "If I say to a woman, 'Give me a drink,' and she says to me, 'Drink and I will give your camels something to drink too,' let her be the one." No sooner than he had finished praying, Rebekah came to draw water. He asked her for a drink and she responded that she would draw water for his camels too.

What kind of woman would do this task? It would not be uncommon to give a drink to a stranger, but to offer to water ten camels is a big task. A thirsty camel can drink up to 30 gallons of water in 13 minutes. Some reports even go as high as saying a 1,300-pound camel can drink 53 gallons of water in three minutes. Whatever the amount is, it seems a camel can have a tremendous thirst after crossing the desert.

Rebekah's offer to water the camels meant that she might have to draw up to 300-530 gallons of water from the well and carry it to the camels. The wells in those days had steps that went down to the water. You would walk down, draw the water, and walk back up with the water pot. Not only was the clay water pot heavy, but a gallon of water weighs over 8 pounds. Imagine a teenage girl carrying even 3 gallons (25.02 lbs.) plus a heavy clay water pot up and down what some have said could have been a hundred or more times. We certainly don't know how many times, but 10 thirsty camels wouldn't be satisfied with a few slurps from a trip or two down to the well. This was an incredibly strenuous and time-consuming task for a young girl. Only someone with a servant's heart would offer to do this for a stranger. Little did Rebekah know that her act of compassionate service would open the door of an amazing reward, making her an heir of all of Abraham's fortune and earning her a place in biblical history.

The Bible says we are just water pots. Paul said it this way, "We have this treasure in earthen vessels (clay pots)." We are nothing; it is what we carry that is everything. We carry the presence of the Lord with us and release it when we have opportunity to serve others.

I love the story of Jesus and the donkey. When Jesus made what we call His "Triumphal Entry" into Jerusalem just before His crucifixion, He told his disciples to go into town and they would find a donkey that was tied up. They were to untie it and bring it to Him. If anyone questioned them they were to say, "The Lord has need of it." This was done in fulfillment of the prophecy.

This is significant because the donkey is just a beast of burden—a servant. Yet it carried the King of Kings and Lord of Lords on his back. The story goes on to say that Jesus went into the temple and the blind and the lame came to him and He healed them. Who was it that carried Jesus to the place of miracles? It was a donkey that became part of the miraculous events, and found a place in the Biblical narrative. You too can find a place in God's narrative as you humbly carry Jesus to where the needs are and compassionately serve people in His name.

Chapter 9

SEVEN KEYS TO GREATER FAITH PART 1

Where Faith Comes From

Jesus was hungry, so He wandered off the road that led from Bethany to Jerusalem because He saw a fig tree in the distance. Nothing like a good fig to fill an empty stomach. But this was not the season for fruit, only leaves.

I just love Jesus' response; it's so very human. Can't you relate? I sure can. "Let no one eat fruit from you ever again." Was He really irritated or simply wanting an object lesson for the next morning? Maybe a little of both. But sure enough, the

> *I* cannot believe that the God who created us and places such an emphasis on faith would not put within us a capacity for faith to seek Him.

lesson from the withered fig tree would give us a profound teaching on faith from the Master.

Jesus responded to Peter's observation of the fateful tree:

> *"Have faith in God. Truly I say to you, whoever says to this mountain, 'Be taken up and cast into the sea,' and does not doubt in his heart, but believes that what he says is going to happen, it will be granted him. Therefore I say to you, all things for which you pray and ask, believe that you have received them, and they will be granted you." Mark 11:22-24*

We've looked at the ingredients necessary for miracles. Now let's examine how to increase our faith for the miracles. I'm as hesitant to list "keys" as I was "ingredients" because moving in faith and miracles is never a formula for man to figure out. I use these words simply as categories to assist us in understanding how we can be in a proper position to see the hand of God. Which brings me back to Mark 11…The word "faith" in the Greek is *pistis*. Strong's #4102 refers to conviction, confidence, trust, belief, reliance, trustworthiness, and persuasion.

But the key to "The Keys" (if you will) is Jesus' initial statement in verse 22, "Have faith IN GOD (emphasis mine)." It always begins there. It's not about faith in our faith, but about the source of our faith—God. It is faith that is rooted completely in Him and His ability.

This may seem self-evident. However, far too often I've seen sincere believers slip subtly into faith in their own faith rather than a reliance and belief in the true object of their faith—Him.

This can lead to pride, self-righteousness, and condemnation to those around who seem to "lack faith." Lives, families, churches, and entire movements can be devastated by this insidious misunderstanding. On the other side, I've seen fear of this happening grip leaders and they abandon a very core ingredient to their daily walk—the exercising of faith in God.

Let's examine and incorporate seven keys to walking in a greater faith.

Key 1: Understand Faith is a Gift

I believe everyone is given a bit of faith in this life. I cannot believe that the God who created us and places such an emphasis on faith would not put within us a capacity for faith to seek Him. Somewhere around the year 1660, Blaise Pascal articulated the idea of a "God-shaped hole" in every person that causes that person to seek after the divine. This inclination to the spiritual, by its very nature, requires faith in some type of spiritual realm and being, be it Baal, Zeus, or Jehovah. In fact, this seed of faith is brooded over and fanned into flame by the Holy Spirit as He works in the life of a believer to bring about conviction of sin, show the need for salvation, and reveal Jesus as the Savior. Just as the Word and the Spirit worked together to miraculously bring the world into existence (Genesis 1:1, John 1:1), the Word and the Spirit work together to generate a faith response to the message of salvation through Jesus Christ. Paul told us in 1 Corinthians 1:21 that God chose the foolishness of preaching (Word) and faith (Spirit) to impart salvation, so that man could not boast in his intellectual prowess or his religious self-righteousness.

Paul reminds us of this fact:

> *For it is by grace you have been saved, through faith—and this not from yourselves, it is the gift of God. Ephesians 2:8 NIV*

> *…as God has allotted to each a measure of faith. Romans 12:3b*

If you are a Christian, you obviously have a measure of faith. Let me ask you this: Do you believe God has a place for you in Heaven? Have you ever seen Heaven? You have never seen Heaven but you believe it is there. Really? Do you believe Jesus died for your sins on the cross of Calvary? Do you believe that the blood shed on that cross was enough to cleanse your sins? So, you haven't seen that cross or that blood, but you believe it made the way for you to have eternal life. Guess what? You have faith! Now your faith needs to grow. It can be cultivated and developed.

In 1 Corinthians 12 Paul lists the nine "gifts of the Spirit." Faith is on the list as a "gift." Now this gift is somewhat different than the measure of faith each has been given. The nine gifts of the Holy Spirit are supernatural empowerments that are given to meet a specific need for a specific time. The gift is the "word of knowledge" or the "word of wisdom," not general knowledge or wisdom. Likewise, this "gift of faith" is a gift limited to a specific situation. However, the point is, it is still called a gift.

A friend of mine tells a story of the first time he operated in the gift of faith. He was directing a school for short-term missionaries in a local church. He and the 150 plus students were all scheduled to go on a dozen or so short-term teams around the world.

They had all put in sizable deposits toward the flights to various nations, but they only had 24 hours to complete the transaction or lose thousands of dollars. My friend gathered his leaders together to seek the Lord. He knew it would take a miracle because they were, as he described it, "all poor college students" and they had to raise thousands of dollars in 24 hours.

As they prayed, the Lord spoke clearly to my friend, "I will give you the gift of faith." He recalled, sheepishly, that at the time he wasn't sure what the "gift of faith" was. Before he shared the word with his leaders, he tried negotiating, "How about the gift of money, Lord?"

But he was obedient even though the other leaders also seemed unsure. Then as they announced the financial challenge to the entire school, faith surged through my friend, "I knew we'd be all right as I spoke to the class."

Sure enough, a joy swept over the school and students began to both give and receive money. For an hour they worshiped, prayed, and gave each other checks and bills. At the end of the time, everyone had their way paid, plus an extra $7,000 to bless the people they would serve.

All of us have been given a measure of faith. All of us have also been given the mandate and ability to grow in faith. How much faith we develop is up to us, although I believe God is constantly at work in our lives to grow our faith. The remaining steps will give us the knowledge and the tools needed to work on cultivating a deeper faith in God.

Key 2: God's Word is Essential to Faith

So then faith cometh by hearing, and hearing by the word of God. Romans 10:17 KJV

If you lack faith, I know where you can get it. It comes to us through the Word of God—the Bible. This is one reason why there is such a satanic attack on the authority and inspiration of the Bible in this day and age. If faith is required to please God, and faith comes by hearing God's word, then if Satan can undermine God's word, he can either keep people from faith or rob them of the faith they have. Either way, he wins. He does not care how religious a person is—in fact, the more religious the better, as far as he is concerned—as long as a person does not develop faith.

We see this principle spoken of in Hebrews as a warning to us concerning the Israelites failing to enter the Promised Land.

> *For indeed we have had good news preached to us, just as they also; but the word they heard did not profit them, because it was not united by faith in those who heard. Hebrews 4:2*

We hear statements like, "The Bible is not the Word of God, it only contains the Word of God." Or, "Men wrote the Bible and it's full of errors so it cannot be God's Word." Or, "The Bible is outdated and not relevant to modern society." Or, "Science has proven the Bible to be wrong, so it cannot be God's Word."

All of these statements seem to be proof positive (at least to the non-believer or nominal believer) that we have no authoritative Word on which to base our faith. For those who choose the "Christian religion," and do not hold an authoritative view of the Bible, the Bible has become a self-help book, or a guide on social consciousness. When this happens, people are left to pick and choose what parts of the Bible they want to accept and believe in, and they disregard the rest. We certainly have a lot of that going on today.

> We must approach God's Word with a firm conviction that it contains the truth of God and the resident power of life.

The really funny thing to me is that these people will adamantly state that the parts about God loving us and wanting to forgive us are really God's words, while the "thou shalt not" parts are just man-made. Don't you think it strange that anything that might deal with man's sinfulness can't be the Word of God?

The bottom line though is that if God has not spoken, there is no basis for faith since "faith comes by hearing God's Word." This is probably one of the biggest reasons why people pray and do not see answers to those prayers—they have never settled the issue in their heart that the Bible is God's Word, and as such, has the character and integrity of God Himself attached to it. Faith in God's Word is truly a faith in the character of the God who spoke the Word and made the promise. Undermine that, and there is no basis for biblical, miracle-working faith.

Of course once a person accepts the Bible as God's Word, there is just something about the power of God's word that always seems to raise their faith levels.

Whenever I hear it, read it, or even speak it myself, it seems that somehow my faith levels just start to rise up. This is exactly what God promises will happen. However, it doesn't just happen with a casual approach to the Bible. There has to be some level of hunger and desire to know, understand, and live God's Word.

People have asked me how I grew in faith. I think it started when I just literally spent night and day cramming the Word of God into my mind and spirit.

When I was just a young Bible college student I found that I really did fall in love with the Word of God. And not just in my studies, but in everything and every way that I could pack it into my brain, heart, and soul. I used to set my cassette tape recorder to record all the preachers on the radio. I would then listen to them while driving to and from my Bible college. I continued to listen after I was home from school and while making my lunch. Even at work I was able to put my headphones on, and instead of listening to music, I listened to more of the Word. Then, when I got home from work I was usually very tired, but would put in another cassette of some preacher screaming out the gospel while I slept.

Even after Bible college I would buy up every tape series I could get my hands on. I would listen to some over and over again. People at traffic lights would sometimes laugh at me as they heard the loud preaching of the Word, rather than the latest top 40. Somehow it found its way into my heart, soul, and spirit.

Jesus told His disciples, "It is the Spirit who gives life; the flesh profits nothing; the words that I have spoken to you are spirit and are life." (John 6:63) We must approach God's Word with a firm conviction that it contains the truth of God and the resident power of life. We absorb that life every time we interact with it in faith.

Key 3: The Impartation of Faith

I have been reminded of your sincere faith, which first lived in your grandmother Lois and in your mother Eunice and, I am persuaded, now lives in you also. 2 Timothy 1:5 NIV

With these words the old apostle encouraged Timothy, the young pastor that he had mentored for so many years. It seems that somehow Timothy's faith started and was imparted to him by the relationship with his mother who had faith and his grandmother who was full of faith.

There is a principle here that is often missed in teachings on faith: You need to be around the right people—people who build you up and encourage you in the things of God. People who have faith will generate faith in others. People who grumble and complain and bemoan their trials will likewise reproduce themselves. Could it be that many preachers actually teach their congregations how NOT to have faith? There are many denominations that have reduced the Bible to a self-help book and teach that God doesn't do the miraculous today.

We see this principle plainly taught in scripture.

> *After seeing Jesus do it, his faith just rose to the occasion.*

> *Blessed is the man who does not walk in the counsel of the wicked or stand in the way of sinners or sit in the seat of mockers. But his delight is in the law of the LORD, and on his law he meditates day and night. He is like a tree planted by streams of water, which yields its fruit in season and whose leaf does not wither. Whatever he does prospers. Psalm 1:1-3 NIV*

> *He who walks with wise men will be wise, but the companion of fools will suffer harm. Proverbs 13:20*

When I think of Joshua, I am confronted with the fact that the miracle he experienced actually impacted the entire earth. Moses saw his staff become a serpent. He saw the Nile River turn to blood. He saw the plagues that swallowed the life of Egypt. He of course saw the Red Sea open for them to cross. But now imagine all of those incredible miracles that took place and yet Joshua was to be instrumental in one that was greater than them all.

> *Then Joshua spoke to the Lord in the day when the Lord delivered up the Amorites before the sons of Israel, and he said in the sight of Israel, "O sun, stand still at Gibeon, and O moon in the valley of Aijalon." So the sun stood still, and the moon stopped, until the nation avenged themselves of their enemies. Is it not written in*

> *the book of Jashar? And the sun stopped in the middle of the sky and did not hasten to go down for about a whole day. There was no day like that before it or after it, when the Lord listened to the voice of a man; for the Lord fought for Israel. Then Joshua and all Israel with him returned to the camp to Gilgal. Joshua 10:12-15*

I really began to wonder…where did Joshua learn that kind of faith? I think something of Moses rubbed off on Joshua after over 40 years of serving and walking with him.

You see the same thing with Elisha, who walked with and served Elijah.

> *When they had crossed over, Elijah said to Elisha, "Ask what I shall do for you before I am taken from you." And Elisha said, "Please, let a double portion of your spirit be upon me." 2 Kings 2:9*

Elisha was just a servant to the prophet, "pouring water on his hands." Yet he spent his days and nights in the shadow of this great man of God. He heard the prophetic words Elijah spoke and the teachings he gave to the school of the prophets. He witnessed the miracles and saw how the man of God lived a life devoted to God. No doubt his faith was greatly challenged and encouraged by being around this man.

You even see this witnessed with Peter when Jesus came to the disciples at the Sea of Galilee walking on the water.

Immediately He made the disciples get into the boat and go ahead of Him to the other side, while He sent the crowds away. After He had sent the crowds away, He went up on the mountain by Himself to pray; and when it was evening, He was there alone. But the boat was already a long distance from the land, battered by the waves; for the wind was contrary. And in the fourth watch of the night He came to them, walking on the sea. When the disciples saw Him walking on the sea, they were terrified, and said, "It is a ghost!" And they cried out in fear. But immediately Jesus spoke to them, saying, "Take courage, it is I; do not be afraid." Peter said to Him, "Lord, if it is You, command me to come to You on the water." And He said, "Come!" And Peter got out of the boat, and walked on the water and came toward Jesus. But seeing the wind, he became frightened, and beginning to sink, he cried out, "Lord, save me!" Immediately Jesus stretched out His hand and took hold of him, and said to him, "You of little faith, why did you doubt?" Matthew 14:22-36

Wow! I know Peter lost it there for a moment and let fear take over, but I am still impressed that he actually tried for a moment to walk on water. Imagine being these experienced fishermen that are scared to death of this figure they thought was a ghost walking in the middle of an unimaginable storm. Think about the fact that Peter was willing to try going out in the midst of this storm toward Jesus. I really have to give Peter some huge credit on this one.

Yes, his faith went down a notch or two for a moment and he sank, but he really did something that I would dare say very few today or throughout history would have tried. Then I thought, where did Peter ever get the idea he could walk on water? I don't think Peter or anyone else in their wildest dreams would have ever come up with something as crazy as that. So, where in the world did Peter ever get the idea that he could walk on water? After seeing Jesus do it, his faith just rose to the occasion.

These examples teach us that faith is imparted to us and cultivated in us by the people we spend our time with. If we spend our time with doubters and those that tend to be negative, we often end up the same way. But I have noticed that people who spend their time with those who encourage them, pray with them, and speak faith and hope into them often take on that same faith themselves.

When I get around great men and women of God, people who have seen many miracles in their ministries, I often ask them to pray for me for an impartation of faith. I want the kind of faith that sees lives changed. I want to see people healed and set free, demons cast out and blind eyes opened, deaf ears made to hear. I want to see the dead raised. I want to be around people who will encourage and challenge my faith—people who want to see the same things I do.

One of the greatest missionaries and evangelists the Foursquare denomination has ever produced was Sister Evelyn Thompson, a petite woman with a powerful voice and ministry. She led thousands and thousands to the Lord, baptized in the Spirit with many getting healed.

Before she ever dreamed of such exploits, the Foursquare founder, Sister Aimee Semple McPherson, laid her hands on the 19-year-old Evelyn and prophesied over her, telling her that she would carry on the anointing, doing even greater things than Sister McPherson.

Can you imagine what that did to this tiny teenager? It could crush a weaker vessel, but not this soon to be powerhouse.

In Sister Thompson's later years, after she had returned from the mission field, Julie and I made a point of visiting her, anticipating one amazing story after another of God's greatness. The last time we saw her, just before her passing to glory, she was particularly excited to hear our stories from Indonesia. This time, before we left, she laid hands on me and prayed and prophesied many things over my life, some of which I am doing now. The anointing was so strong that even after several days it seemed I could barely walk under the anointing that she carried.

Surround yourself with people of faith. Yet, gently encourage those with weaker faith—always in love.

Chapter 10

SEVEN KEYS TO GREATER FAITH PART 2

Things You Can Do to Build Your Faith

Key 4: Pray in the Spirit

Leslie fell asleep, exhausted from hours of ministry in Papua New Guinea. When the Lord woke him at 3:00 a.m. to pray, he resisted. The flesh was winning.

But because Dr. Leslie Keegel, a nation changer with an apostolic ministry, is a man of God, he relented. Well actually, according to Leslie, also a humble and honest man, it took the Lord a second time, literally pushing him out of bed before he would pray!

And pray he did, mostly in tongues, for an hour until the Lord brought a person's name to him. He prayed for

> *W*alking in faith has a lot to do with understanding what God is doing and what your part is in that plan.

this person in tongues for another hour until the burden lifted.

Two days later, in Sydney, Australia, Leslie was speaking in church when a person came up to him after the service. This person introduced himself, but Leslie knew exactly who he was. "I've been praying for you in tongues. What's going on?" The man told how he had separated from his wife and that tomorrow the divorce would become official. Leslie encouraged him, albeit briefly. "Don't worry. God is in control. The burden has left me."

That evening Leslie spoke at another church and his topic was forgiveness. While speaking about bitterness and how it will destroy you, a woman rose up from her chair and left the church. Leslie thought she was either angry or resisting the Spirit. But after the service she explained to Leslie that she had to call her husband immediately and tell him that she was not going to divorce him. She had forgiven him. She asked him to forgive her—all because God spoke to her during Leslie's message. They were reconciled.

Through praying in the Spirit, Leslie had great faith to trust the Lord for this man's situation—enough faith to speak to this person in a way some of us might even consider dismissive. In Leslie's heart the battle had been won the night before—it was just a matter of God's timing.

The great evangelist, Smith Wigglesworth, saw hundreds and some say thousands of miracles in his ministry, even many raised from the dead. People would often come to him and ask, "Brother Wigglesworth, what is the secret to your powerful ministry?" One time he simply replied:

> *But you, dear friends, build yourselves up in your most holy faith and pray in the Holy Spirit. Jude 1:20*
>
> *A person who speaks in tongues is strengthened personally. 1 Corinthians 14:4 NLT*
>
> *He that speaketh in an unknown tongue edifieth himself. 1 Corinthians 14:4 KJV*

The word "edify" in the original language means to lay a foundation for building, to erect a house, or to repair a house. The truth is that you can build yourself up in the faith. You can activate the faith that you have, and increase it if you want to. You can lay a foundation for growing your faith. You can even repair spiritual damage done in your life. The personal gift of tongues is given for that very purpose. Yet relatively few use it with that in mind.

One of the ministries of the Holy Spirit is to teach us the things of God. Walking in faith has a lot to do with understanding what God is doing and what your part is in that plan. Jesus said, "I only do what I see the Father doing." Jesus indicates that He did not do his miraculous works on His own volition, but rather as He understood and cooperated with the divine plan and purpose for His life and for the lives of those He ministered to.

Jesus told his disciples that they were His friends because He shared with them all the Father's plans. Now it is the Holy Spirit's job to impart to us the plans and purposes of God.

> *However, as it is written: "No eye has seen, no ear has heard, no mind has conceived what God has prepared for those who love him"*—**but God has revealed it to us by his Spirit.** *The Spirit searches all things, even the deep things of God. For who among men knows the thoughts of a man except the man's spirit within him? In the same way no one knows the thoughts of God except the Spirit of God. We have not received the spirit of the world but the Spirit who is from God, that we may understand what God has freely given us. 1 Corinthians 2:9-12 NIV*

It is unfortunate that most preachers stop at the end of verse 9 and start talking about Heaven and how we can't possibly imagine all the glories that await us. And I am sure that is true. But this passage isn't about Heaven or what we don't know and can't understand about the future. It is about what we CAN know and understand by revelation. When you read seamlessly from verse 9 to 10 you discover that we can't know and understand the things of God with our natural human abilities, but we can know them by revelation of the Spirit.

Paul and Jude indicate that using the gift of tongues in prayer facilitates this impartation of spiritual knowledge and wisdom.

Out of all of the nine Gifts of the Spirit, the gift of tongues is the most controversial. Protestant churches have been more divided over this than any other subject. It might be good to demystify the subject a little bit by understanding that "tongues" just means "languages." It is the supernatural impartation of the Holy Spirit to speak a language that someone has not learned naturally.

Because the gift of tongues is both a critical step of growing faith and one of the most controversial subjects in the Bible, I have included a section that deals with some questions and objections that some people have about the gift of tongues. This will hopefully be clarified even more as it is explained more thoroughly in Chapter 12.

Key 5: Take Steps of Faith

Since faith is spiritual and not natural, and because it comes from "hearing God's Word," it is quite possible for anyone to start out seeing incredible miracles. However, many of us just coming into this revelation are growing from "faith to faith"—that is, as we express our faith in small areas and gain confidence for greater things.

Early in our ministry, we would take bags of food to minister to the poor in our community. As people would gather, we'd share the Word. One time after sharing the story of Jesus touching the woman with the issue of blood, a transient woman asked me, "Would He touch me too?" She had chronic pain in her leg, adding misery to an already difficult life. After we prayed she began to shout, "The pain is gone! The pain is gone!"

This really encouraged me to believe for even "bigger" miracles throughout my life.

We see this principle expressed in the Bible. Goliath taunted the armies of Israel and every warrior was shaking in their sandals. However, David had already experienced the supernatural protection and enablement of the Lord in his life. He drew on his previous faith encounters to rise up and meet the current challenge.

> *Then Saul said to David, "You are not able to go against this Philistine to fight with him; for you are but a youth while he has been a warrior from his youth. But David said to Saul, "Your servant was tending his father's sheep. When a lion or a bear came and took a lamb from the flock, I went out after him and attacked him, and rescued it from his mouth; and when he rose up against me, I seized him by his beard and struck him and killed him. Your servant has killed both the lion and the bear; and this uncircumcised Philistine will be like one of them, since he has taunted the armies of the living God." And*

> *David said, "**The Lord who delivered me from the paw of the lion and from the paw of the bear, He will deliver me from the hand of this Philistine.**" And Saul said to David, "Go, and may the Lord be with you."*
> 1 Samuel 17:33-38 [emphasis mine]

You probably have had faith encounters of your own when you stop to consider what they really are. Those answers to prayer we often take for granted are the little steps of faith that lead to greater encounters and answers. Remember the bill that needed to be paid and the money came in unexpectedly? Or the headache that you forgot you had after you prayed? What about that bad report from the doctor, or lawyer, or mechanic that seemed to loom so large and it turned out to be something small in the long run? All of these "lions and bears" are meant to build your faith for the "Goliaths" of life.

In the self-centered application of faith—which is mostly about me getting what I want—love has no place, unless it is self-love.

One situation is no more difficult for God than another. Cancer is no more difficult for God to heal than a headache. Your need for $10,000 is no bigger a problem to God than your need for $100. Use those previous blessings as a launching pad for greater miracles.

Key 6: Ask for More

Seeing a demon manifest is nothing to look forward to. I find it interesting that American believers are so fascinated with the subject. Over the years, I've probably seen it all, even an "Exorcist-like" head turning 360 degrees (what I've been told…I've never seen that movie). All the strange voices, smells, and contortions are done to inspire fear and chase away faith. Usually these tactics work to the opposite on me, stirring compassion and an eagerness to see freedom for the person in bondage.

Once, in Fiji, a 19-year-old woman, well-dressed, attractive, and sitting with everyone else in church, manifested a demon during worship. She went through the usual contortions and was foaming at the mouth. I am very careful when ministering individually to a woman, so I let the ladies of the church attempt to cast the demon out.

Unfortunately, they were not very successful and my daughter came to me, pleading for me to "do something." I thought about it, wondering why these godly women were having such trouble. I even doubted myself for a moment until I asked the Lord, "God, give me more faith for this!"

I jumped in front of this poor young woman, rebuked the evil spirit, and commanded it to leave. She began to come back to normal, cleaned up, and returned to the service.

Sometimes we just have to ask for more faith.

> *The apostles said to the Lord, "Increase our faith!" He replied, "If you have faith as small as a mustard seed, you can say to this mulberry tree, "Be uprooted and planted in the sea," and it will obey you. Luke 17:5-9 NIV*

What stands out to me is that Jesus never rebuked the disciples for asking for their faith to be increased. Because of this I am convinced that it is okay for you to ask for your faith to grow on a daily basis. Faith is a key ingredient to both our spiritual lives and to seeing miracles. I encourage you to pray for an increasing faith on a daily basis.

Jesus wanted the disciples to grow in faith. I believe He was pleased with the revelation they came to: 1. They wanted and needed a greater level of faith. 2. It was not something they could manufacture for themselves. However, the disciples seemed to miss something that Jesus corrected. The disciples asked for more faith (quantity) and Jesus corrected them and helped them to understand that they needed a greater faith (quality). His statement, "If you had faith…" isn't an indictment that they had none, for we have already seen that God has dealt everyone a measure of faith. But rather, it points to the quality of their faith.

There is one verse that speaks about the quality of our faith, and it is often overlooked in typical teachings on faith—and that for an obvious reason.

> *For in Christ Jesus neither circumcision nor uncircumcision means anything, but faith working through love. Galatians 5:6*

Real faith doesn't give up.

Faith works by love. In the self-centered application of faith—which is mostly about me getting what I want—love has no place, unless it is self-love. However, a faith motivated by self-sacrificing love for others will move mountains.

The apostle James dealt with a question the church had: "Why aren't our prayers getting answered?" His reply was twofold: 1. You didn't ask. 2. You asked for the wrong reasons and with the wrong motives. (Notice he didn't say they asked for the wrong things.)

I have known many people who wanted a healing ministry for their own ego's sake. While God occasionally honored the faith (quantity) they had, they rarely saw the results they claimed or expected. Often they would explain away unanswered prayer by blaming the person they were praying for as not having enough faith. "Be it unto you according to your faith," makes a great escape clause when things don't happen.

Perhaps the key to "greater faith" is the purification of our motives.

Jesus repeatedly taught His disciples to ask for what they needed.

> *So I say to you, ask, and it will be given to you; seek, and you will find; knock, and it will be opened to you. For everyone who asks, receives; and he who seeks, finds; and to him who knocks, it will be opened. Now suppose one of you fathers is asked by his son for a fish; he will not give him a snake instead of a fish, will he? Or if he is asked for an egg, he will not give him a scorpion, will he? If you then, being evil, know how to give good gifts to your children, how much more will your heavenly Father give the Holy Spirit to those who ask Him? Luke 11:9-13*

In this teaching, Jesus specifically tells us that God will give us more of the Spirit when we ask Him to. The implication is that if we ask for a good thing, He won't substitute something bad.

> *If you abide in Me, and My words abide in you, ask whatever you wish, and it will be done for you. My Father is glorified by this, that you bear much fruit, and so prove to be My disciples. John 15:7-8*

In the context of a teaching on how to be an increasingly fruit-bearing Christian, Jesus drops this most astounding promise: Whatever you need to be FRUITFUL, you can ask for and have assurance of receiving. Too often this verse is quoted out of context and all we hear is, "Whatever you ask for in my name the Father will give to you." However, the conditions were abiding in Christ and bearing fruit for God.

Now the most obvious question is, "Would more (quantity and quality) faith make you more fruitful?" Of course it would. So the obvious solution is to ask, seek, and knock for faith to be more fruitful in ministering to others.

Key 7: Never Give Up! Persistent Faith

We had an amazing woman of faith in our congregation in California. She was Jewish and her parents had lived in England while the millions of other Jewish people were suffering not so far away during the Holocaust of World War II. One Sunday, she came to me and asked for prayer for her mother to be saved. Her mother was a very sweet lady but did not believe in Jesus. The daughter believed that God had promised her that her mother would be saved. She continued to come week after week asking for prayer for her mother. I finally thought, "God, if this is going to happen, you better get on the stick before her mother dies."

I still remember the day when Julie and I were at our house not far from where they lived. All of a sudden we started hearing sirens coming down the street. We heard several different sirens from emergency vehicles and I thought something very bad must have happened.

This woman's mother used to go for walks around her block. It was a busy street and the traffic moved along at a good speed. On this day she stepped off the curb in front of an oncoming car. At 45 miles per hour the driver had no time to react and hit her. Many people saw the accident and saw her frail body fly into the air and land several feet away. The driver of the car was traumatized even though there was nothing he could have done to avoid it. Everyone was sure she was dead.

When the sirens came, the daughter ran outside and somehow just knew that it was her mother. As she ran to the scene of the accident, the police would not let her go to her mother's body. Finally, the paramedics came over and said, "Your mother is still alive, but we haven't moved her yet. She keeps saying something over and over and over again." They brought the daughter over to the mother and she asked her, "Mother, are you okay." Her mother replied, "I saw Him." She said, "Excuse me mother, what did you say?" Then over and over again, the woman kept repeating the same thing, "I saw Him! I saw Him!"

The paramedics said that was all she had been saying. The daughter asked, "Who did you see?" The mother replied, "I saw Him, I saw Jesus. I saw His robe."

The daughter asked if Jesus had said anything to her. She replied, "Yes, He said, 'Daughter, it is not your time.'" She got up off the street absolutely unharmed. It is a miracle that she survived at all. She had been hard of hearing, which may have been a factor in the accident, but afterward her hearing was restored.

This woman, in her nineties, not only accepted Jesus as her Savior, but began to boldly tell people about Him and witness to the miracle in her life and to share the message of Jesus Christ the Savior. She may have brought more people to the Lord in the rest of her life than her daughter had in all the years prior to her mother's conversion.

The daughter's faith was strong. She believed what God had spoken to her. It didn't matter how long it had been or how old her mother was getting, she believed the promise. She was consistent and persistent to come to the altar every Sunday to ask for prayer, believing her mother would come to Jesus before she died. She just didn't give up.

Real faith doesn't give up. We have already looked at those Old Testament saints who "died in faith, not having received the promise." We have the testimony of Job the righteous, who said, "Though He slay me, yet will I trust Him." And then there is Abraham, who left his home and family and started a journey that had no definitive end as far as he could see. He was willing to be obedient, even to the point of sacrificing his son.

This is significant, not only because of the extreme of obedience, but because every promise God had made to him was to be fulfilled through the son whom he was to sacrifice. To obey God in sacrificing his son meant that he was effectively sacrificing every promise God made to him. Can you see this amazing paradox of faith? The Bible said Abraham didn't stagger at the promise. His conclusion: Since

God was true to His word, the only possible alternative was that God would raise Isaac from the dead. (Hebrews 11:19)

This scripture encourages us to not give up, and provides us with some practical wisdom about how to shore up our faith. The first principle is wholehearted trust. Half-hearted trust doesn't go very far. God told Israel, if you search for me with your whole heart, you'll find me. Being half-hearted doesn't get you half of God—it gets you nothing.

We have to come to the place where we believe that God will lead and guide us, even if we don't always understand what is happening in our lives. This level of trust isn't something that comes naturally or without decision. Often a person comes to the place where they have to make a decision: Am I going to trust God or not? With this decision comes the peace we were looking for before we made the decision.

The second principle is acknowledging God in all our ways. This simply means that, to the best of our ability, we are seeking God's guidance and yielding to His will in every area of our lives. Many people make their plans and ask God to bless them without ever consulting the Lord about His will.

James echoed this principle in the New Testament:

> *But if any of you lacks wisdom, let him ask of God, who gives to all generously and without reproach, and it will be given to him.* ***But he must ask in faith without any doubting, for the one who doubts*** *is like the surf of the sea, driven and tossed by the wind.* ***For that man***

ought not to expect that he will receive anything from the Lord, being a double-minded man, *unstable in all his ways.*
James 1:5-8

Chapter 11

THE POWER OF PRAYING IN THE HOLY SPIRIT

But you, dear friends, build yourselves up in your most holy faith and pray in the Holy Spirit.
Jude 1:20 NIV

I spent all of my early years in the Methodist church where those precious saints led me to Jesus and took care of me during those troubling years of my early life. However, I had never heard about the Gift of the Holy Spirit or speaking in other tongues as the early believers did in Acts chapter 2.

When I first started in Bible College I began hearing more and more about this gift. I was so hungry for everything God had for me, and when I realized that I was missing something, the hunger grew even more.

After class one day I went to Pastor Richard Casteel and

> "Dad, I don't think that's the Devil. My friend does that as well and I think it's beautiful."

asked if he would pray with me for this incredible gift. He of course was happy to and laid hands on me and instantly I was filled and began speaking with other tongues, though only a few words at first. I was so excited that I went home and got on my knees and prayed in tongues for at least a few hours. It seemed like the more I prayed in the Spirit the more it seemed to flow out of me like a river. With this new gift I was absolutely on fire for God and eager to tell anyone and everyone what had happened to me.

When I was a teenage boy my father had left and my mother was with her new husband driving a semi tractor trailer cross-country. I was mostly left to care for myself. During that time there was an older gentleman that took me under his wing. After I had wrecked the car I had spoken about in Chapter 1, this man gave me another car that he had just sitting on his property. He always tried to help and encourage me to go forward in life—that is, until I was baptized in the Holy Spirit and started praying in other tongues.

I drove over to his house one morning. When he saw me he could tell I was excited and had joy written all over my face. He said, "You look happy, what's going on?" I told him the story of my journey with God and how the Holy Spirit had filled me.

Immediately his countenance changed and he looked sternly at me and said, "You didn't speak in tongues, did you?" I said, "Oh, yes I did!" He then said, "Let me hear it."

In all joy, I began to speak in that new language from Heaven. Then he stopped me. He turned in anger and said, "You didn't get the Holy Spirit, you've got the Devil. The Devil has filled you!"

With that, he called in his daughter and said, "Listen to this. Jerry got filled with the Devil." His daughter responded back to her father and said, "Dad, I don't think that's the Devil. My friend does that as well and I think it's beautiful." He still insisted saying, "No, that is the Devil."

My great joy turned to sadness that day when I realized I had lost a friend. I never saw him again after that and heard he died of cancer not long afterward. It was so sad to me that a man who always professed to be a Christian died never experiencing the beautiful gift of the Holy Spirit.

The Gift of Tongues (Languages)

There are several arguments people use to dismiss tongues as a valid gift for today.

But are they valid arguments?

1. **It's not for today, it went when the Apostles died.** Two thousand years of ancient church history, and more specifically, the last 115 years of modern church history provide abundant proof that this is simply not so. According to a seminar given by Allen Anderson at Wheaton College in April 2014, there were 631 million Pentecostals in 2014

comprising nearly one quarter of all Christians worldwide. In 1970, there were only an estimated 63 million. The world-wide total of Christians embracing Pentecostalism is expected to reach 800 million within 10 years.

2. **Paul said, "When that which is perfect has come, that which is part shall be done away with."** Those dismissing the gift of tongues state emphatically that the Bible is the "perfect" thing that was to come and that tongues was temporary and only necessary until we had a completed Bible. The only problem with that is that you have to force an interpretation of what "that which is perfect" means. Paul did not say "the Bible." In fact, there is no indication that Paul knew there would be a "Bible" as we know it. There are quite a few legitimate interpretations of what this might mean. For instance, "that which is perfect" may mean the "salvation ready to be revealed in the last time," spoken of by Peter in 1 Peter 1:5 and by John.

"Dear friends, now we are children of God, and what we will be has not yet been made known. But we know that when he appears, we shall be

like Him, for we shall see Him as He is."
(1 John 3:2 NIV)

We cannot build or refute a doctrine based on an oblique scripture requiring a personal interpretation.

3. **Well, Paul asked the question, "Do all speak in tongues?"** Isn't Paul indicating that not everyone would speak in tongues? Yes, but that same Paul said, "I speak in tongues more than all of you." He also said, "I would like every one of you to speak in tongues …" (1 Corinthians 14:5) and "…do not forbid speaking in tongues." (1 Corinthians 14:39 NIV)

4. **It sounds like that couldn't be a language.** I have visited every continent, other than Antarctica, and have heard all kinds of different languages that may sound strange to someone who speaks English only. Some of the tonal languages of East Asia sound so different to Westerners that we could think they couldn't be a language at all. By the way, the most dominant personal tongues sound the same no matter what native language is spoken, and I've heard thousands and thousands of people all over the world.

5. **Well it wasn't supernatural; it was just languages that people didn't know and others just translated for them.** Paul said it was the language of both "men and angels ..." (1 Corinthians 13:1) He also said, "For anyone who speaks in a tongue does not speak to people but to God. Indeed, no one understands them; they utter mysteries <u>by the Spirit</u>." (1 Corinthians 14:2) Hazel Thompson, an American missionary working deep in Africa, was praying for a seven-year-old girl to receive the baptism of the Holy Spirit. When the Holy Spirit filled her she heard this African girl praising God in English with an American accent.

I remember another story about a soldier who was serving in Japan. He married a Japanese woman and brought her home. He started going to church, and though his wife did not believe in Jesus, she went with him to honor him. One day he responded to an altar call and went to be prayed for. His Japanese wife went with him, and while standing beside her husband she became aware of another man standing near who was worshiping in the Spirit and praying in tongues. She then heard the words in her language, "You have tried

Buddha, and you have tried Zen, why not try Me, My name is Jesus Christ." Let me ask you, do you believe in Jesus? Do you really believe?

Jesus said speaking in "new tongues" was the sign that you believed in Him.

> *And these signs will accompany those who believe: In my name they will drive out demons; they will speak in new tongues. Mark 16:17 NIV*

It is both strange and unfortunate that most people who claim the gift of tongues is not for today get their information about it from people who do not speak in tongues. If you want to understand about the gift of tongues, it makes more sense to talk to someone who has experienced it.

Think about all that Jesus said before he went to Heaven.

Speaking about the outpouring of the Holy Spirit that was documented in Acts chapter 2, He said,

> *And I will ask the Father, and He will give you another Helper, that He may be with you forever; that is the Spirit of truth, whom the world cannot receive, because it does not behold Him or know Him, but you know Him because He abides with you, and will be in you. John 14:16-17*

> *When the Helper comes, whom I will send to you from the Father, that is the Spirit of truth, who proceeds from the Father, He will bear witness of Me, and you will bear witness also, because you have been with Me from the beginning.*
> John 15:26-27

The word "helper" here is *paracletos*, meaning, "One who comes along side of you to help."

> *But you shall receive power when the Holy Spirit has come upon you; and you shall be My witnesses both in Jerusalem, and in all Judea and Samaria, and even to the remotest part of the earth.* Acts 1:8

The word for power here is the Greek word *dunamis*. It is the word from which we get dynamite; an explosive, forceful power. It is a small thing that causes great destruction. What if tongues are a small thing that cause great destruction to the enemy?

We have to see how important this is.

> *And when the day of Pentecost had come, they were all together in one place. And suddenly there came from heaven a noise like a violent, rushing wind, and it filled the whole house where they were sitting. And there appeared to them tongues as of fire distributing themselves, and they rested on each one of them. And they*

were all filled with the Holy Spirit and began to speak with other tongues, as the Spirit was giving them utterance. Acts 2:1-4

What was the very first thing he had them do when they received the Holy Spirit in the upper room? They spoke in other tongues. Have you ever asked why? Have you ever wondered why they didn't prophesy or lay hands on one another or worship or preach? Why, of all nine spiritual gifts listed in 1 Corinthians 12, did God choose this one as an initial manifestation of the Spirit? I believe it is because this gift is the personal gift that edifies and builds a person's faith to live for and serve God.

A person who speaks in tongues is strengthened personally…1 Corinthians 14:4 NLT

He that speaketh in an unknown tongue edifieth himself…1 Corinthians 14:4 KJV

To edify means to build up. So speaking in tongues allows a person to "build himself up."

I remember talking to a pastor who was working in a particularly difficult area. He related how missionaries and pastors would come and go regularly. The witchcraft in this area was so strong that the missionaries would last only a few months. Then he made this statement, "Where I live you have to pray at least one hour a day in the Holy Spirit just to survive."

So how does this work? How is praying in words you can't understand supposed to build you up?

> *And in the same way the Spirit also helps our weakness; for we do not know how to pray as we should, but the **Spirit Himself** intercedes for us with groanings too deep for words. Romans 8:26 [emphasis mine]*

From his own experience, Paul relates that we often don't know how to pray as we should. We can run out of things to pray about in five minutes. I have heard many people say they just don't have anything to pray about.

Truly we don't know how to pray as we should. Many times our limited understanding of the situation or our idea of how a prayer should be answered actually hinders the answer, because we cannot see all the spiritual details about the things we are praying for.

Continuing on, Paul says:

> *And He who searches the hearts knows what the mind of the Spirit is, because He intercedes for the saints according to the will of God. And we know that God causes all things to work together for good to those who love God, to those who are called according to His purpose. Romans 8:27-28*

We tend to quote verse 28 every time something goes wrong in someone's life. There is always some dear brother or sister trying to encourage someone that their tragedy is really the will of God that He is working for their good. The truth is, that isn't how that verse actually works. If you read the verses above and below you get the context. This is for those who are praying in the Spirit because the Spirit knows how to pray God's perfect will into a person's life. It is also reserved for those who "love God and are called according to His purpose."

Of course God will work all things together for the good in those situations, because God's will for us is always good when we respond to God's call on our life, seek to serve Him, and trust the Holy Spirit to guide, enlighten, and empower us.

I remember a story of a pastor who was engaged and preparing for his wedding. The date was set and everything was in order when his fiancé decided to call off the wedding. He was so upset about it that he didn't know what to do. He really believed that it was the Lord's will for them to be married. A few months went by and she met another man and got engaged to him. He said the Lord woke him up one morning and said, "I want you to pray for your former fiancé, but pray in the Holy Spirit." I think he was a bit reluctant to do so because of the feelings he had and the fact that she was engaged to someone else. However, he obeyed. And as he was praying in tongues the phone rang and

Did Jesus ever have a prayer that was not answered?

sure enough it was her. She said, "I don't know what happened, but the Lord just spoke to me and said that you were the one I was supposed to marry. You are truly the one the Lord has for me." She broke off the engagement to the other man and married the pastor and they went on to minister together.

As we pray in the Spirit our faith is built up and we start to believe for things that we couldn't believe for before. Think about Peter. On the night before the crucifixion he denied that he even knew Jesus. But on the Day of Pentecost, after speaking in tongues by the power of the Holy Spirit, he stood up before the multitude and preached the first Christian sermon and 3,000 people got saved.

We don't always have the time to pray according to our knowledge. However, if you will make a priority of praying in the Spirit, the Spirit will intercede for you and work all things according to God's will.

My schedule is so hectic that I don't have time to stop and pray as much as I really need to sometimes. However, I have learned to pray in the Spirit whenever I can. When I am walking through an airport, driving in the car, or standing in a line, I can pray in the Holy Spirit and know that those prayers are perfectly aligned with God's will. A few minutes of praying in the Holy Spirit may often

> ...Some of the nuns, fell under the power of the Holy Spirit.

be more effective than an hour praying in our own wisdom and understanding or according to our own wants and wishes.

Consider this: Did Jesus ever have a prayer that was not answered? Of course not, because he always prayed according to the Father's will. Even when we as the people of God pray according to His will, we have the promise of receiving.

> *This is the confidence which we have before Him, that, if we ask anything according to His will, He hears us. And if we know that He hears us in whatever we ask, we know that we have the requests which we have asked from Him.*
> *1 John 5:14-15*

So if even in the natural we pray according to the will of God and are assured results, how much more if the "Spirit Himself" prays for you? If the Spirit of God always makes intercession for us according to the will of God, then every time you pray in the Spirit things are bound to happen. The Spirit is praying through you and praying God's own will. Why wouldn't you want to spend more time praying in the Spirit?

Miracles will just start showing up as you pray in the Spirit. As you pray and obey, you will find yourself right in the middle of what God is doing—sometimes without even knowing it. When you do, the power and authority will flow through your life as you yield to God.

One of the greatest experiences I have ever witnessed took place while ministering on Grande Terre, one of our beautiful South Pacific Islands. I had been speaking all week long for usually at least eight hours or more a day. By the end of the week, I was just about completely out of energy and voice for anything more.

There was one more major event planned for the evening. It was a Friday night outreach for the people in the community. However, it seemed I was so tired from all the giving out that week that I just felt I couldn't go on for another service. I had a real conviction that I should be praying for the upcoming service, but was just too exhausted to mentally or physically work on the words to pray. So, as I always do when feeling too weak to do anything else, I began praying in the Holy Spirit.

It seemed for the next two hours or so that all I could do was to walk around my hotel room and let the Holy Spirit do the work. Finally, I showered, put on a suit, and headed off to the evening meeting. This was to be my last service before heading back to Australia in the morning.

When I arrived, I noticed there were several Catholic nuns in the facility, which I found out later was because this building was rented from them for the night and the nuns were there to keep an eye on us to be sure we didn't get too wild. The pastors escorted me to my seat where I actually fell asleep during the worship service. I can hardly count the times in my life where I have been this tired.

This particular group often would go on for 1½-2 hours in their worship service, which is a wonderful practice and shows their great love for the Savior. However, with my weariness, I was ready for it to end so that I could just get to my sermon, finish my last service, and then get some sleep before my early flight home the following day. Finally, I heard my name announced and realized it was time for the Word. I gave one of my shortest sermons ever as I was determined to get out of there as soon as possible.

Knowing this group of believers and their passion for a touch from God, I knew they would want me to pray and prophesy over all of them. This I knew would keep me there to easily after midnight. Again, because of my weariness, I knew I just wasn't up to it. So I decided to just pray a corporate prayer over all of them. I told them all to stand, lift their hands, and get ready to receive directly from the Holy Spirit. With that, I prayed and then in faith said, "Get ready, Jesus is going to touch you now." To my absolute amazement almost everyone in the building, including some of the nuns, fell under the power of the Holy Spirit. This was the first time that evening that I really woke up and God had my attention.

From this beautiful display of the Holy Spirit reaching into and touching the lives of these hungry believers I felt it was a good time for me to leave and simply let God do the work He intended for that evening. With that, I grabbed my Bible and headed for the door.

The pastor who drove me wanted to know where I was going? I said, "Brother, I am so tired. Could you please take me back to the hotel?" He immediately responded, "Oh, no brother, that's out of the question. There are still so many to pray for." I said, "I don't need to pray for anyone, look around. The Holy Spirit seems to be touching them all." He said, "Yes, but do you see all those people along that wall?" As he pointed to the left side of the building he said, "All those came tonight because we advertised that you pray for the sick, and they have all come with special needs. Pastor, I won't take you back until you pray for them." I thought to myself, "This is going to take all night."

With this new challenge I knew there was no way I was going to get out early that night. And being that they spoke another language and each prayer need would have to be interpreted to me and then me back to them, I expected it to be a really long night. Then it came to me that I would not give the time to hear their prayer request, but rather trust the Holy Spirit to do the work.

Since I didn't understand them and they didn't understand me I started at one end of the line and just started laying hands on them, praying in the Holy Spirit and in English for each one of them.

All of a sudden one of the leaders started shouting, "Look at the blue water! The water is so beautiful and blue coming out of you onto the people."

I really didn't feel a thing and no one was displaying anything that appeared to be a touch from the Holy Spirit. I continued working my way down the prayer line, toward the exit door, hoping that I could leave after this time of prayer.

Finally, I came to the end of the line where there was a young boy—I'm guessing 11-13 years old—standing with crutches. One of his legs was all bandaged up and the blood was coming through in what looked like a rather primitive job of bandaging his wound. Apparently, he had run across a street in front of a truck and a tire caught his leg before getting to the other side.

The boy looked to be in horrible pain and misery. However, this time something very evident happened when I prayed. At the moment I touched him there was the audible sound, that all of those around could hear, of the bones coming back together and the leg being instantly healed. This boy started shouting, "The pain is gone, the pain is gone!" Praise God for His love and compassion for this hurting young boy.

The next morning four pastors came very early to pick me up to take me to the airport for my flight back to Australia. While driving they were all talking amongst themselves.

I couldn't understand them but they seemed very excited about something. I finally asked,

> "*I* thank my God I pray in tongues more than all of you."

"What's going on, why are you guys so excited?" With that, one of them responded back to me in English, "We have been up all night hearing the testimonies from all the people you prayed for at the end of the service." He then told me the words that brought me tears of joy: "Every person you prayed for last night was healed."

That day I learned one of the greatest lessons in all of my years of ministry—always trust the Holy Spirit to do a much better job than I could ever do in my own strength or through my own understanding of the needs.

I have since always made it my habit to pray in the Holy Spirit before and during every meeting and trust that as I do He is planning and doing things according to His will.

That experience taught me that if we will always give what we have and do our best, God will do what we cannot do in our own strength. This gave me a whole new understanding of Paul's statement, "for when I am weak, then I am strong." (2 Corinthians 12:10b)

God has promised to give you the wisdom and knowledge you need to minister effectively to people through the Holy Spirit. You need to believe this and trust this promise as you step out in faith to minister to others.

> *No, we speak of God's secret wisdom, a wisdom that has been hidden and that God destined for our glory before time began. None of the rulers of this age understood it, for if they had, they would not have crucified the Lord of glory. However, as*

it is written: "No eye has seen, no ear has heard, no mind has conceived what God has prepared for those who love him"—but God has revealed it to us by his Spirit. The Spirit searches all things, even the deep things of God. For who among men knows the thoughts of a man except the man's spirit within him? In the same way no one knows the thoughts of God except the Spirit of God. We have not received the spirit of the world but the Spirit who is from God, that we may understand what God has freely given us. This is what we speak, not in words taught us by human wisdom but in words taught by the Spirit, expressing spiritual truths in spiritual words. 1 Corinthians 2:7-15

Do you wonder how I can be this bold? I pray in the Spirit a lot! I pray in the airport, in the car, walking through a store, in church. Paul told the Corinthian church, "I thank my God I pray in tongues more than all of you." Could it be that the secret to Paul's incredible ministry was this simple discipline—praying in tongues?

The gift of tongues is literally for God to keep you strong, move you into His will, and reveal the plans and purposes of God to you. I don't know how you can live without it.

Chapter 12

RECEIVING THE INCREDIBLE GIFT OF TONGUES

I looked out from the stage upon at least a thousand young faces. Over the last few years I've been blessed to see a true revival happening among the young people in the South Pacific, Papua New Guinea, and Indonesia. Tens of thousands have been saved, filled with the Spirit, and are witnessing their faith.

This time I simply asked the question to this group of eager, beaming youth: "How many of you have received the Holy Spirit?" I counted only eight hands. So I asked them another question: "How many of you want to receive power from the Lord?"

With that, they began to run to the altar, all of them, many falling to the ground and speaking in tongues. No begging, no extended music. There was no laying on of hands, no instructions, no separate prayer room—just kids filled and enjoying the very presence of God.

Early in my ministry, I would have mocked this story if a missionary dared to tell it in my church. I'd laugh at people slain in the Spirit on television. I'd become comfortable as a pastor/teacher. Until one day, my wife asked me, "Honey, what has happened to you? You used to be so passionate for the move of God."

She was, of course, right. But it would take a few years at a well-known and ongoing revival meeting for something to happen.

To this day, I don't remember anything specific or spectacular, just that I left that meeting with a tremendous love for people, much more than ever before. And I couldn't stop praying in tongues.

> *And they were all filled with the Holy Spirit and began to speak with other tongues, as the Spirit was giving them utterance. Acts 2:4*

It is important to remember that the "gift of tongues" is one of the "gifts of the Holy Spirit." Some people make the mistake of seeking the gift and not the giver. However, in the verse above we find they are intimately connected; the gift flows—perhaps overflows—from the giver. To seek the gift alone is often the reason why people don't receive it.

The Holy Spirit works in and through us as we develop an intimate, cooperative relationship with Him. When a person seeks a deeper relationship with the Holy Spirit by seeking and receiving the baptism of the Spirit, it generally results in the manifestation of the gift of tongues since, as we have already discussed, tongues was a gift primarily used for personal edification and strengthening. It only makes sense then that this is the first gift a person experiences as they enter into the new dimension of spirit-filled living. In Papua New Guinea, it is natural to see people emerge from the waters of baptism speaking in tongues.

A Faith Issue

Like everything else in the Christian life, the baptism of the Holy Spirit and all of the gifts of the Spirit are accessed by faith. That is, a person believes a promise from God and receives it for themselves through faith. We are saved that way. We are healed that way. We interact with the Spirit that way. God wants you to be filled with the Holy Spirit and has promised it to you.

> *Gathering them together, He commanded them not to leave Jerusalem, but to wait for **what the Father had promised**, "Which," He said, "you heard of from Me; for John baptized with water, but you will be baptized with the Holy Spirit not many days from now." Acts 1:4-5 [emphasis mine]*
>
> *For the **promise** is for you and your children and for all who are far off, as many as the Lord our God will call to Himself. Acts 2:39 [emphasis mine]*

Notice two significant things in these verses. The outpouring and infilling of the Holy Spirit were specifically "the promise of the Father." Peter later picks up on this theme and extends that same promise to "…all who are far off," meaning everyone else in the entire world—from those who heard him speak to those living in the end of the age.

As we have already seen, there are a number of questions and objections that some raise concerning the baptism of the Spirit and the gift of tongues. When a person has unresolved questions or false beliefs they tend to struggle with releasing faith. I have discovered that once a person's questions or false impressions have been answered or corrected, faith is released and the believer receives the baptism in the Spirit and the gift of tongues easily.

Ask

> *For everyone who asks, receives; and he who seeks, finds; and to him who knocks, it will be opened. Now suppose one of you fathers is asked by his son for a fish; he will not give him a snake instead of a fish, will he? Or if he is asked for an egg, he will not give him a scorpion, will he? If you then, being evil, know how to give good gifts to your children, how much more will your heavenly Father give the Holy Spirit to those who ask Him? Luke 11:10-13*

It is unfortunate that some churches teach that someone who speaks in tongues is worshiping the devil. They even have their favorite missionary story to tell along with it.

However, when you ask God for something good, He is not going to give you something bad.

> God doesn't give bad things to those who ask Him for something good.

The parallel passage to the one above, found in Matthew chapter seven, says exactly the same thing with one obvious difference. Instead of the phrase "Holy Spirit," Matthew uses the phrase "good things." So we can conclude that the Holy Spirit is a "good thing." We can also conclude that the gifts of the Holy Spirit are good things. After all, He is God's Spirit. The apostle John says, "Every good and perfect gift comes down from the Father of lights." (James 1:17)

A pastor friend of mine tells his own story of when He was filled with the Holy Spirit and spoke in tongues for the first time:

> *In 1980, at the age of 20, I was born again in a Fundamental, Independent Baptist Church. We were taught that Charismatics, Pentecostals, and other "Spirit Filled" people were not Christians and, in fact, had demonic spirits. Anyone who spoke in tongues was worshiping the devil. Needless to say, we never talked to that "spirit filled" group, but avoided them like the plague.*

There was a blind lady in our town that ran a Christian bookstore. Being blind, she personally has a huge library of cassette tapes from the top Charismatic teachers of the day. She loaned these tapes out through her bookstore. Being a good Baptist I frequented the bookstore and became friends with her. After a while she began to share with me the reality of the baptism of the Holy Spirit and speaking in tongues. I was skeptical, but I was interested.

Since my family was going on a road trip for Christmas I asked her if I could borrow some tapes. She later told me she prayed over every tape she loaned me, asking God to open my eyes and speak to me about the ministry of the Holy Spirit.

I had dropped my young family off with my wife's mother to spend a week with her. I was alone on the three-hour drive home and decided to listen to some of the tapes I had borrowed. I popped in one tape, and then another. By the second one God had spoken to my heart and I found myself sitting alongside of the road crying profusely. I had told God that I loved Him and wanted to serve Him, but I didn't want the gifts He had for me. When I realized I was spurning something God wanted me to have, I broke down and repented. That day I truly believed in the baptism of the Spirit and speaking in tongues, but had not yet received the evidence, being that I was still having a problem with all the negative teaching I had received.

When I returned home I shared my story and asked my friend if I could talk to her pastor. The pastor came to my home and when I opened the door I said, "I am interested in the Baptism of the Holy Spirit, but because of my theological background, you have some convincing to do."

For over an hour he patiently answered my questions and tried to help me overcome the objections I had been taught. It came down to a decision on my part. The whole demonic thing was a concern to me. Could I trust God?

It was then the pastor shared these two passages in Matthew and Luke with me, pointing out that one said God would give "good things" to those who asked, and the other said God would give "the Holy Spirit" to them who asked.

At that point my wife and I asked him to lay hands on us and pray for us to receive the baptism of the Holy Spirit and the gift of tongues. As he began to pray I prayed to God,

> *"Father, I am asking you for a good thing. I am not asking the devil for anything. If this is not of you, and it is indeed a bad thing, I don't want anything. I trust you." Almost immediately I started speaking in another language and my wife did as well."*

God doesn't give bad things to those who ask Him for something good. If you are struggling with the validity of the Spirit-filled life, open your heart and trust God to give you something good. Truly God's gifts are good gifts.

Have Someone Who is Filled with the Spirit Pray for You to Receive the Spirit

> *Now when the apostles in Jerusalem heard that Samaria had received the word of God, they sent them Peter and John, who came down and prayed for them, that they might receive the Holy Spirit. For He had not yet fallen upon any of them; they had simply been baptized in the name of the Lord Jesus. Then they began laying their hands on them, and they were receiving the Holy Spirit. Acts 8:14-17*

Jesus told His disciples to go out and minister to the masses. He said, "Freely have you received, freely give." I cannot give what I don't have. I can give what I do have. A

Spirit-filled believer can pray and impart the Holy Spirit to another believer. In this way the gospel is "viral"; that is, it is passed from one believer to another, much like our discussion on faith being imparted by those we hang around with.

While there are many instances of people being spontaneously filled with the Holy Spirit without anyone even being around, we also have ample evidence from the scriptures that the Spirit was imparted through the laying on of hands.

A minister friend told me how he had struggled for several years on the issue of tongues. He was at his wit's end when he cried out to God, silently during a Bible study.

Sitting alone and not near anyone, he told the Father, "For the last time, Lord, if you want me to be prayed for, for tongues, have someone tap me on the shoulder!" The meeting was just about to close when the tap came on his shoulder. He turned around to see who did it, but no one was there. However, he got prayer that evening from a very godly man who laid hands on him and gently led him to receive his heavenly language. "He was the perfect person to pray for me. The Lord knew who I needed."

How Much You Get is Up to You

For He whom God has sent speaks the words of God; for He gives the Spirit without measure.
John 3:34

God has not placed a pre-determined limit on how much of the Holy Spirit can and will operate in your life. Just as your faith can increase, so can the measure of the Holy Spirit in your life. This works in two ways.

First, as we open our hearts and lives to more of the Holy Spirit's influence and power, we will see a greater moving of the Spirit in our life.

> *The baptism of the Holy Spirit was not meant as an optional element of the Christian life that a person could take or leave at their personal whim and will.*

It is possible to develop faith in one area and not in another. For instance, a person might have developed faith in the financial realm, but struggle with faith for healing. As a person continues to grow in God's word and bring other areas of their life under the control of the Spirit, they will see a greater impact of the Spirit in their life.

Second, as we allow the Spirit to flow through us in greater freedom, we will see a greater manifestation of the Spirit around us. Fear, timidity, pride, self-righteousness, and other "fleshly" things will hinder the free flow of the Holy Spirit through us to others. As we allow the process of sanctification in our lives, we will also see a greater and more consistent flow of the Holy Spirit outward in ministry.

Ask for a Refill

While there is an initial infilling or baptism of the Holy Spirit, we should not think of it as a one-time experience. On the Day of Pentecost, the 120 in the upper room were filled with the Holy Spirit and spoke in other languages. Later that same group of people were all filled with the Holy Spirit again. We read the report in Acts chapter 4. The apostles had just been threatened with beatings and imprisonment if they continued to witness about Christ.

> *"And now, Lord, take note of their threats, and grant that Your bond-servants may speak Your word with all confidence, while You extend Your hand to heal, and signs and wonders take place through the name of Your holy servant Jesus." And when they had prayed, the place where they had gathered together was shaken,* ***and they were all filled with the Holy Spirit*** *and began to speak the word of God with boldness. Acts 4:31* [emphasis mine]

I have always found it interesting that the early church did not pray for safety. Look at what they did pray for: boldness and miracles. In response to that prayer, the place was shaken with the power of God and they were all filled again with the Holy Spirit.

In Acts 13:52 we are told, "And the disciples were continually filled with joy and with the Holy Spirit."

God is calling His church to arise, to awaken from its slumber.

Paul told the Ephesian church not to be "drunk with wine, wherein is excess; but be filled with the Spirit." (Ephesians 5:18) The Greek word here means to "make replete." Literally it means to cram a net to its capacity or to fill up a hollow space. A Spirit-filled Christian can (and needs to) experience occasional refilling in their endeavor to walk in the Spirit.

Understand the Importance of the Spirit-filled Life

The baptism of the Holy Spirit was not meant as an optional element of the Christian life that a person could take or leave at their personal whim and will. Edification, joy, peace, revelation, power, sanctification, and answered prayer are all wrapped up in this issue of the baptism of the Holy Spirit.

> *But if the Spirit of Him who raised Jesus from the dead dwells in you, He who raised Christ Jesus from the dead will also give life to your mortal bodies through His Spirit who dwells in you. Romans 8:11*

Ted Olbrich and his wife, Sou, who are literally transforming the Buddhist nation of Cambodia, believe the missing ingredient in many American Christian lives is that they fail to continually and faithfully speak in tongues. In Cambodia, it is a core Kingdom principle and has given the average Cambodian believer power to overcome challenges most Americans could never imagine. Miracles and healings are all part of the everyday walk in Christ. According to Dr. Olbrich, to not teach or practice the speaking in tongues would be "Spiritual Malpractice. No one believes in the power of tongues more than I do!!"

A Last Word

What will win the world for Christ? More relevant churches? More celebrities coming to Christ? More good books? I suppose none of these could hurt. In fact, the church should always seek excellence in whatever field it plows.

God is calling His church to arise, to awaken from its slumber. I've seen it already happening around the world—young and old, rich and poor.

The common ingredient of these powerful moves of His Spirit is just that—His Spirit. And the common conduit is His people. Not just the "pros" or the educated, or even the trained, but simply folks who "position" themselves to receive and then go, receive and then go, again and again.

Because we all are jars of clay and therefore leak, we are only as good as our last filling. The rest of the world seems to get that. Maybe it's because they are not as filled up with so many other things and there is a profound sense of need.

My sincerest prayer is that the U.S. church is not left behind in what I believe is a final wave coming. I wrote this book because I know the Lord will only use those who are surrendered to Him and empowered by Him.

Let's arise, Church, and position ourselves for battle. May it start with us.

ABOUT THE PUBLISHER

Foursquare Missions Press was founded in 1981 with the purpose of providing free Gospel literature to the world. To date, this ministry has distributed over 195,000,000 pieces of literature to 114 countries in 60 languages. In August of 2002, the Press established a training and resourcing ministry to children's workers around the world. The Children's Gospel Box ministry assists thousands of children's workers and children annually. Over 500,000 children have come to Christ and have been discipled. Missions Press is a non-profit organization supported by the gifts of its friends. For more information, visit our website at:

www.foursquaremissionspress.org

[**Please note:** No donor funds were used to publish this book.]